Embark on a Journey of Enablement:

I magine you are going on a trip. You know where you want to go, but you're not sure how to get there. You need a map or a guide to help you through the twists and turns of the road ahead. In the business world, empowerment is like a plan. Imagine that you are going on a trip. You know where you want to go, but you're not sure how to get there. You need a map or a guide to help you through the twists and turns of the road ahead. In the business world, empowerment is the road map that gets you to your goal of success.

I0479243

Foreword

In the competitive business world of today, it's not enough for companies to give their workers the information and skills they need to do their jobs. They also need to give them the tools they need to reach their full potential and help the organization do well. This is where being in charge comes in.

Enabling is the process of giving people and groups the knowledge, tools, and resources they need to do their jobs well and improve their performance. But it's not enough to just give help and training; you also need to set up the right tools and methods and create an environment that supports growth and development.

This book goes into detail about what enablement is and how it works. It takes readers from a basic understanding of the idea to how enablement programs can be used in a company. This book is a big change from standard performance management to people support. It shows how important it is for adults to keep learning and growing throughout their lives.

The book shows the different ways adults can learn by showing best practices in teaching design based on a deep understanding of the market. It goes into detail about the most important parts of successful enablement programs, like how important cross-functional teams are and how ongoing enablement is better than event-based enablement. The book then goes into detail about the methods and performance of enablement, focusing on how important content management and measurement are to making enablement projects work. It gives good tips on how to reach people by using games and changing the way they think. It also warns about common mistakes that can make support efforts fail. Lastly, the book gives practical tips on how to lead and promote enablement within an organization. It tells readers how to build a good reporting system and measure the success of enablement. The book ends with a deep look at the important role of enablement in the workplace today and the constant need to improve and advance enablement programs.

CHAPTER 1:

Introduction

Before we set out on our journey, we need to understand what enablement is and why it's so important. In this chapter, we'll define enablement and discuss its benefits.

Insights from the Market

- Every successful journey begins with research. In this chapter, we'll take a look at the current state of the market and examine the trends and challenges that businesses are facing.

Shifting from Performance Management to People Enablement

To truly enable people, we need to shift away from traditional performance management practices. In this chapter, we'll explore why this shift is necessary and what it means for businesses.

CHAPTER 2:

Children VS Adults

- Learning Everyone learns differently, but there are some key differences between how children and adults learn. In this chapter, we'll examine these differences and discuss how they impact enablement.

How People Learn

- To enable people, we need to understand how they learn. In this chapter, we'll take a deep dive into the science of learning and explore the different types of learning styles.

Adult Learning Techniques

- Based on what we've learned about how adults learn, we'll explore the best techniques for adult learning and discuss how to apply them to enablement.

CHAPTER 3:

Understanding Enablement
- In this chapter, we'll define enablement and discuss the different aspects of the enablement process.

Enablement Focuses
- Enablement isn't a one-size-fits-all approach. In this chapter, we'll explore the different areas of focus for enablement and discuss how to tailor enablement to meet specific needs.

The Breakdown
- In this chapter, the importance of understanding the components of enablement is emphasized. Enabling employees involves providing them with the necessary knowledge, skills, tools, and support to perform their roles and contribute to the business's success.

The Team
- Enablement is a team effort. In this chapter, we'll discuss the different roles involved in enablement and how to build an effective enablement team.

Cross-functional teams
- Enablement often requires cross-functional collaboration. In this chapter, we'll explore how to build effective cross-functional teams and discuss the benefits of collaboration.

The Structure
- Enablement needs a solid structure to be successful. In this chapter, we'll discuss the different structures that can be used for enablement and how to choose the right one for your organization.

Continuous Enablement vs Event Enablement

- Enablement is an ongoing process, not a one-time event. In this chapter, we'll discuss the difference between continuous enablement and event enablement and why continuous enablement is crucial.

Timing

- Timing is everything when it comes to enablement. In this chapter, we'll discuss how to time enablement initiatives for maximum impact.

Logistics

- Enablement requires careful planning and execution. In this chapter, we'll discuss the logistics of enablement and how to ensure a smooth delivery.

Instructional Design

- To create effective enablement programs, we need to apply instructional design principles. In this chapter, we'll discuss the basics of instructional design and how to apply it to enablement.

Breaking Down Barriers and Silos

- To truly enable people, we need to break down barriers and silos. In this chapter, we'll examine the common barriers to enablement and discuss how to overcome them

CHAPTER 4:

Enablement supporting new HR trends

- The world of HR is constantly evolving, and enablement needs to adapt to these changes. In this chapter, we'll discuss how enablement can support new HR trends, such as remote work and diversity and inclusion initiatives.

Enablement Methods

- Enablement can take many different forms. In this chapter, we'll explore the different methods of enablement, such as coaching, mentoring, and e-learning.

Execution

- To make enablement a success, we need to execute our plans effectively. In this chapter, we'll discuss how to ensure smooth execution of enablement initiatives.

CHAPTER 5:

Content Management

- Enablement requires a lot of content. In this chapter, we'll discuss how to manage enablement content effectively and ensure that it's accessible to those who need it.

CHAPTER 6:

Reach People Through Games

- Games can be a powerful tool for enablement. In this chapter, we'll discuss how games can be used to engage learners and reinforce learning.

CHAPTER 7:

Mindsets

- To enable people, we need to cultivate a growth mindset. In this chapter, we'll discuss how to promote a growth mindset and why it's important for enablement.

Enablement Pitfalls

- Enablement isn't always easy. In this chapter, we'll discuss common enablement pitfalls and how to avoid them.

CHAPTER 8:

Measurement

- To know whether our enablement efforts are working, we need to measure their impact. In this chapter, we'll discuss how to measure enablement effectiveness and use the data to make improvements.

CHAPTER 9:

You & Enablement

- Enablement isn't just for managers and trainers. In this chapter, we'll discuss how individuals can take ownership of their own enablement and drive their own development.

CHAPTER 10:

Leading Enablement

- To make enablement a success, we need strong leaders. In this chapter, we'll discuss the qualities of effective enablement leaders and how to develop these skills.

CHAPTER 11:

What if no enablement is done?

- In this chapter, we'll explore the consequences of not prioritizing enablement and discuss why it's crucial for businesses to invest in enablement initiatives.

CHAPTER 12:

Selling Enablement Internally

- Getting buy-in for enablement initiatives can be a challenge. In this chapter, we'll discuss how to sell enablement internally and get stakeholders on board.

CHAPTER 13:

Reporting Structure

- Enablement needs a solid reporting structure to be effective. In this chapter, we'll discuss the different reporting structures for enablement and how to choose the right one.

CHAPTER 14:

Points of Enablement

- Success To make enablement a success, we need to celebrate our wins. In this chapter, we'll discuss the different points of enablement success and how to recognize and celebrate them.

CHAPTER 15:

The Future of Enablement

- The world is constantly changing, and the future of work is no exception. In this final chapter, we'll discuss what the future of enablement might look like and how businesses can prepare for it.

Chapter16:

Final Thoughts

- Our enablement journey may be coming to an end, but the learning never stops. In this chapter, we'll reflect on what we've learned and discuss how to continue to improve our enablement efforts.

CHAPTER 1

Introduction

Humans have succeeded because they've been able to learn and adapt. Learning has always been crucial, from the days when young ones picked up survival skills from their parents to today, where we create complex tools and societies. This drive to learn and improve isn't just about individual growth; it's essential for society's progress too.

Humans learned by mimicking what they saw, which helped them evolve. Early humans picked up tool-making, food-finding, and safety tricks from their elders.

As people learned more, they developed the ability to think and reason, leading to advanced communication and problem-solving techniques. Eventually, this evolved into sophisticated practices like farming, writing, and career advancements.

Learning matters a lot because it helps us survive and succeed in life. It equips us with the knowledge and skills needed to adapt to our environment, tackle challenges, and thrive.

It's also crucial for personal and professional growth. By learning, we can sharpen our abilities and pursue our interests and passions. Plus, it can help us advance in our careers and achieve our workplace goals.

Learning is super important for society to advance. It helps people pick up new ideas and tools, which sparks innovation. Plus, it makes individuals more aware and respectful of their surroundings, enabling them to benefit everyone.

In the business world, empowering employees is key to success and achieving company goals. It means giving workers the knowledge, skills, tools, and support they need to excel and help meet overall objectives.

Good support programs can boost job performance, productivity, customer satisfaction, and business growth. By focusing on enabling their staff, companies provide them with resources to thrive in a fast-changing business environment.

Today's competitive market makes enablement more crucial than ever. Rapid changes will keep happening, and businesses that don't adapt will fall behind. To stay relevant, investing in employees and equipping them properly is essential.

However, some companies overlook the importance of enabling their workers. They fail to invest in providing necessary support, leaving them at a disadvantage in today's intense market competition.

Ignoring employee support has high costs. Without proper enablement programs, staff may lack the information and skills to perform well, leading to poor performance, lower productivity, and unhappy customers. This can result in underperformance and a weaker market position.

Businesses not prioritizing enablement will struggle to survive the next five years as industry changes accelerate. Staying relevant requires investing in your workforce and ensuring they have what they need to succeed.

Investing in enablement isn't just about improving staff performance and productivity. It's also about positioning the business for long-term success. By continually equipping employees with the necessary knowledge, skills, and tools, businesses can foster innovation, satisfy customers more, and boost long-term sales and profit.

To be successful with support, businesses need to take a whole-person approach that considers both the needs of the business and the needs of each employee. This means making complete programs that give workers the help they need to do well in their jobs and the tools and resources they need to keep learning and improving over the course of their careers.

INSIGHTS FROM THE MARKET

Marketers and sellers used to work on their own, without much help from each other: Marketers and sellers often had different goals and key performance indicators (KPIs), and they didn't work together much. Marketing focused on making campaigns and events, while sales focused on turning the leads that these efforts brought in.

Because the buyer's journey is so complicated these days, marketing and sales need to work together more: Because the modern buyer's journey is getting more complicated, marketing and sales need to work together closely to create and keep a steady stream of income. This means that both groups must work toward the same goal and use the same success measures.

Because of this change, jobs have merged: The need for marketing and sales to work together more closely has led to a blurring of jobs within these businesses. Now, CMOs get paid based on how many deals they close, and salespeople are taking on marketing tasks like starting their own mini-marketing campaigns.

For this change to happen, we need technology: For this shift to work, companies need to have technology in place that lets marketing and sales work together in this way.

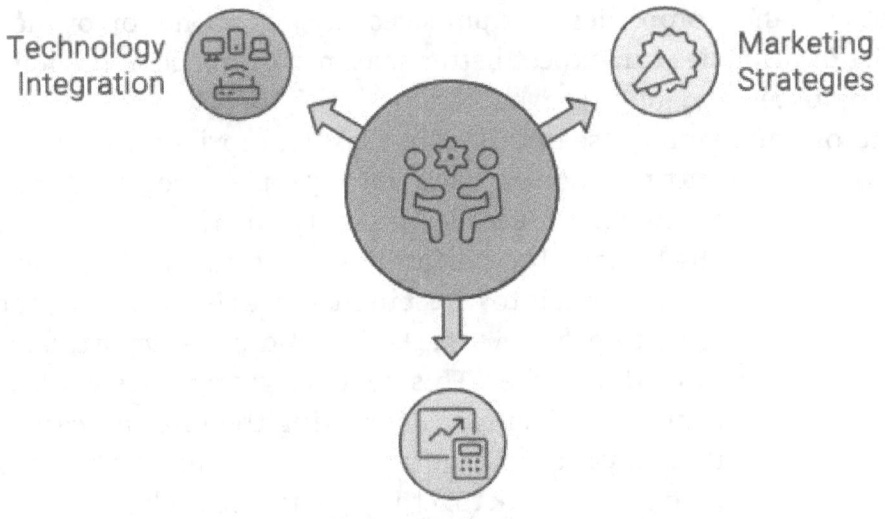

Those who try this method first do better: Research shows that people who use this method early on are more likely to be successful. This means that businesses are more likely to succeed if they can adjust to the new way that marketing and sales work together.

Enabling is a key part of driving organizational change and putting plans in place that are matched with the market. It means looking into the whole process of change and how it affects all parts of a company. This includes analyzing the current sales process, finding areas for improvement, and giving sales reps training and support to make sure they are ready to handle the new strategies. Companies that focus on enablement can create a funnel of change enablers to help facilitate the necessary behavior changes and make sure that all employees are aligned with the new goals and objectives.

It's important to remember that workers won't understand anything that doesn't make sense from a training standpoint. This means that it is important to think about the role of support in any change management process if you want it to work.

Companies that don't put money into sales training may find it hard to get the results and changes in behavior they want. On the other hand, companies that put sales support at the top of their list of priorities can expect better sales performance, more loyal employees, and long-term success.

According to some research, Best-in-Class enterprises are:

- Putting money back into people, processes, and technology to get the most out of marketing and sales alignment: Top-performing businesses know how important it is to invest in their people, processes, and tools to get their marketing and sales departments to work together. This includes giving sales workers training and support, analyzing the sales process to find ways to make it better, and using new tools to help people work together and talk to each other.
- Paying attention to sales content and messaging: One of the most important parts of aligning marketing and sales is making sure that sales reps have access to the right content and messaging to talk to buyers in an effective way. Instead of using traditional methods like flyers and PDFs, the best businesses are using dynamic assets and tools to create content for each buyer while still keeping the brand's identity.
- Giving buyers dynamic assets and tools to make their purchases unique while keeping the brand's integrity: This makes sure that the messages are current and get to the right people while still staying true to the company brand.
- Providing a closed-loop conversation platform for jointly refining messaging: Top-performing companies not only give their sales workers the right material and tools, but they also use closed-loop conversation platforms to help their sales teams improve their messaging together. This process of making changes over and over again makes sure that the wording is effective and speaks to buyers.

- Taking care of channel marketing enablement, marketing operations, and asset management: Top-performing companies also take care of channel marketing enablement, marketing operations, and asset management to help marketing and sales work together. This means making sure that the outlets for marketing and sales are in sync and that

SHIFTING FROM PERFORMANCE MANAGEMENT TO PEOPLE ENABLEMENT

P eople often think of performance management as a way to control and direct employee behavior. However, the focus should be on helping and empowering workers. People Enablement is the name for this method.

For a company to have a People Enablement mindset, it is important to build trust, alignment, and support. This can be done by talking to workers openly and honestly, having clear goals and expectations, and giving them the tools and help they need to do well. In a People Enablement culture, employees are encouraged to take responsibility for their work and given the freedom to make choices and act in ways that support the company's purpose. This gives people a sense of meaning and drive, which can make them more productive and interested in their work. Also, giving workers ongoing training and growth opportunities can help them grow and get better at what they do. This can help people keep their jobs and move up in their careers. This can help people stay with the company longer and move up in their careers, which is good for the organization's general success.

The 5 considerations for enablement success

1. It's important to know the organization's goal and direction so that you can write a clear, meaningful purpose, vision, and values statement that motivates workers through enablement. This can be done by getting the staff involved in making the statement and making sure it fits with their own goals and values. Through enablement strategies like training and support, employees can learn how their jobs add to the success of the company as a whole and how important it is for their actions to be in line with the company's purpose, vision, and values.

2. It's important to match employee goals with

business goals through support if you want your business to be successful and your employees to be engaged. This can be done by giving workers training and support to help them understand the company's purpose and how their jobs fit into it, as well as open communication and clear data to promote employee input and ownership. Among other enablement techniques, regular check-ins and progress reviews can make sure that employee goals are in line with company goals and that any hurdles are quickly taken care of.

3. By giving employees' growth and development top priority, enablement can promote a culture of excellence and development. By giving employees' growth and development top priority, enablement can promote a culture of excellence and development. This can be accomplished by providing employees with the training and support they need to grow in their careers and identify their areas of excellence, as well as the tools and resources they need to be more effective and successful in their jobs. As employees develop and change in their roles, mentoring and coaching programs can also offer direction and support, fostering a culture of ongoing learning and development.

4. By treating every employee with respect and encouraging connectedness and engagement, enablement can create an open and transparent environment. This can be done by giving staff members a chance to talk about their thoughts and fears, as well as by communicating frequently and getting feedback. Training and support are two empowerment tactics that can help the company build trust and openness and give workers a feeling of value and support in their jobs.

5. For employees to move up in the company and do well, it's important to invest in their career growth. This can be done in a number of ways, such as by giving staff members chances to learn and grow, by working with them and their managers to set and support individual job goals, and by giving staff members the tools and support they need to meet their goals. By making professional development through support a top priority, organizations can build a culture of ongoing learning and growth that is good for both workers and the business as a whole.

CHAPTER 2

CHILDREN VS ADULTS LEARNING

Children and adults have very different ways of learning. Adult learning theories take into consideration that adults already have a lot of knowledge and life experience while learning that is geared toward children focuses on giving them a core of knowledge and teaching them how to think critically. They look for ways to keep learning based on their own hobbies, wants, and needs, and they are driven to do so because they know why they are learning. In adult learning, the job of "teacher" can be filled by a guide, coach, training facilitator, friend, or subject matter expert. It can be helpful to let adults figure things out and organize themselves.

Components of Effective Adult Learning

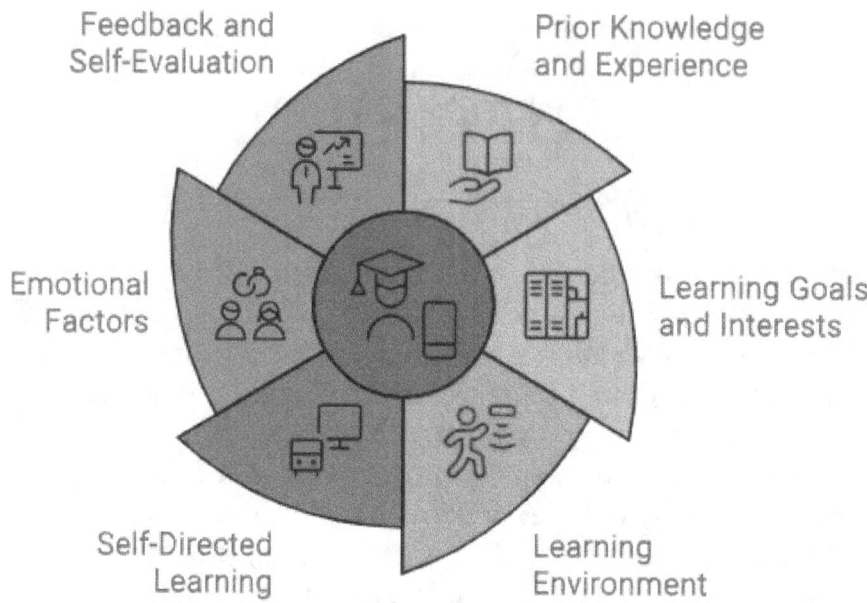

To facilitate learning, it is crucial to involve individuals in the learning process and understand what motivates them. This entails creating a learning environment that caters to the needs of adult learners and providing opportunities for them to engage in meaningful and relevant learning activities aligned with their goals and interests. This can be achieved by designing training programs tailored to the requirements of adult learners or supplying them with tools and support to pursue self-directed learning at their own pace.

For adults to acquire new knowledge effectively, they must have autonomy and the ability to make their own decisions. Adults often need to explore new concepts independently and identify their preferred learning methods. This could involve providing access to online courses, literature, articles, and other educational resources to aid their learning and development.

The key to supporting adult learners lies in acknowledging their individuality, diverse objectives, motivations, and learning styles. By offering a supportive learning environment and the necessary resources, organizations can foster growth, development, and achievement among their employees.

Adult learners face unique challenges and approaches when it comes to education and training. These include emotional baggage, life experiences, intrinsic motivations, and cognitive traits.

Let's briefly examine these aspects.

Adult learners frequently encounter obstacles that hinder their efforts to acquire new skills and knowledge. These difficulties often arise in professional settings where training is a standard method of learning for adults.

Most employees are willing to allocate only 5% of their time to training, making it challenging to prioritize and maintain focus on learning. External factors such as noisy work environments, household responsibilities, and smartphone distractions can also impede concentration during training.

Employees who lack clarity about their roles, feel undervalued, and do not understand how their work contributes to the organization may perceive training as irrelevant. It is essential to communicate the importance of training and development for personal growth and its benefits to the organization. Without this context, employees might not grasp the purpose or expectations of the training.

Engaging adult learners requires clearly explaining the training's objectives and its relevance to their personal or professional lives. If the goals are vague or misaligned with the audience's needs, they may struggle to comprehend and derive value from the training.

Imposter syndrome is another common concern among adults who fear they lack the knowledge to take on new roles or career paths. This anxiety is often exacerbated by fear of criticism and can lead to debilitating self-doubt. Educational theories and psychology models focusing on adult learning in the workplace aim to enhance our understanding and support of adult learners' growth and development. While there is no one-size-fits-all theory about adult learning, each approach provides valuable insights into different facets of the learning process.

Encourage critical thinking by inviting students to provide feedback, share their perspectives, discuss outcomes, and draw their conclusions. Introduce self-assessment practices so students can monitor their progress and set personal goals.

Provide autonomy by incorporating elements of self-paced and self-directed learning into the daily routine, empowering individuals to take control of their educational journey.

Finally, make an emotional connection with learners. Aim to engage them emotionally and stimulate their intellectual processes while delivering practical information. Practice is key.

How people learn

As adults, we learn in many different ways, and our tastes and styles depend on many things, such as our life experiences, goals, and reasons.

Malcolm Shepherd Knowles was one of the first people to work in the area of adult education. He is best known for his theory of andragogy, which is about how adults learn and teach. Knowles thought that adults have different ways of learning and different needs, so he came up with a set of guidelines to guide the creation and delivery of education for adults.

Here are some of these principles:

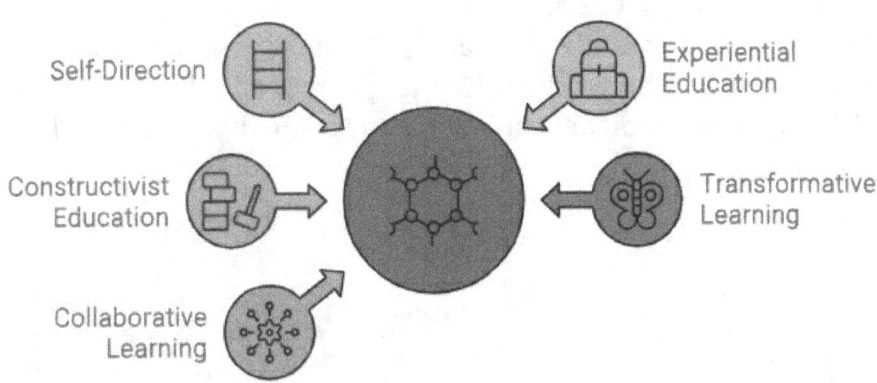

Key Principles of Effective Adult Learning

Self-Direction Learning

As adults, we tend to be self-directed and take care of our own schooling. We look for ways to learn that fit with our own goals and wants, and we are more driven to learn when we feel like we are in charge of it.

Experiential Education

Adults learn best by doing, and when we learn something new, we often draw on what we already know and have done. We are more likely to remember and use new information if it is connected to things we have done or seen in the real world.

Constructivist Education

Adults tend to build their own understandings of new knowledge instead of just taking it in and accepting it. Meaningful learning is more likely to happen when we can connect new information to what we already know and have experienced and when we can actively build our own understanding of the material.

Learning that Changes Lives

Adults are more open to learning that leads to change and growth in themselves. Meaningful learning is more likely to keep us interested when it questions our current ideas and beliefs and helps us grow and develop as people.

Learning Through Collaboration

The best way for adults to learn is to work together and share ideas. When we can work with other people to find out about and talk about new information and ideas, we are more likely to learn something useful.

Adult Learning Techniques

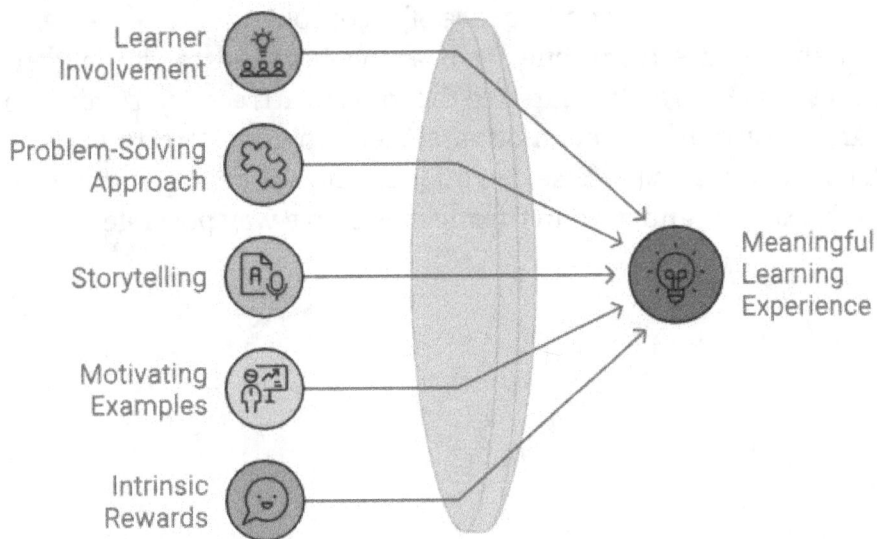

- To increase engagement in adult learners, it is important to consider the psychology of learning and emotions. Here are some techniques that can help facilitate a meaningful learning experience:
- Involve learners in the planning of their education. Allowing adults to choose their own learning objectives has been shown to increase motivation.
- Make it more like problem-solving. Allow your students to concentrate on the problem that can be solved with training or even in the process of learning.
- Make up a story. Use storytelling elements to introduce characters who will accompany learners on their journey to overcome certain challenges related to the new topic.
- Give motivating examples. Share stories about others who participated in training and the outcomes they achieved.

- Experiment with intrinsic rewards to stimulate. Extrinsic motivation is important, but it's also critical to position your training to experience the joy of learning and a sense of accomplishment.

You should use techniques that are well-suited to the learning material and directly related to the topic to attract and retain your learners' attention and motivate them to complete the course. Keep in mind that these techniques should be appropriate for adult learners and used in the most effective way possible.

CHAPTER 3

Understanding Enablement

I t is widely claimed that culture and behavior are the key determinants of corporate performance. This means that a company's culture and how its workers act can have a big effect on how well it can reach its goals and aims. With this in mind, it is very important for companies to focus on helping their workers change the way they act. This can be done in a number of ways, such as through training, help, and advice, and by making the workplace a good place where people want to learn and grow.

Focusing on behavior change can help companies create a mindset of learning and getting better all the time. This can help employees get the skills and information they need to do their jobs well, and it can also help the company change and adapt to meet changing business needs. Traditional training methods, on the other hand, are still useful, but they might not change people's behavior as much or lead to long-term success as well.

Companies should put a high priority on helping people change their behavior because it can lead to success and help build a culture that is upbeat and flexible. Companies can set themselves up for long-term success by investing in the growth of their workers and making the workplace a good place to work.

Enablement is more than just training; it's what makes a company successful. During my career, I've seen a lot of support programs, and the vast majority of them didn't work. A few projects did stand out, but they didn't last long because the empowerment train didn't get enough money or help to keep going.

It is important for support teams not to try to be the "hero" or the go-to source for all information and knowledge in a company.

This is because support teams are often small and don't have the tools or skills to know everything about everything. Instead, enablement teams should focus on making the most of the skills and knowledge of their team members to plan and carry out the organization's support goals.

The best support teams know that the company has a lot of knowledge and experience and work to use this information to make the business successful. One example is making training and development programs with the help of subject matter experts from within the company. This could mean working with experts in the company to create training and development programs or with teams and departments to find places where support could be helpful.

Even though it is important for a company to use the knowledge and experience of subject matter experts, it is also important to be careful when choosing resources for training and development programs. Even if someone knows a lot about a subject, that doesn't mean they are the best person to talk about or teach that topic.

To find the best tools for training and development programs, you should think about a number of things, such as the speaker's knowledge, ability to explain complicated ideas clearly, and ability to connect with and interest the audience. Also, think about how much experience the speaker has running training and development programs and how well they can help and guide pupils in the real world.

Enablement Focuses

The goal of enablement is to help sales teams find and talk to potential customers, as well as give them the knowledge and tools they need to sell a product or service successfully.

But "enablement" can mean almost any position in a company that includes talking to customers, stakeholders, or other people from the outside. This is because every role, no matter what its main goal is, helps the company and its customers create value.

For example, customer service reps are supposed to help customers solve problems and find answers to their questions, which can make customers happier and more loyal. Marketing teams come up with campaigns and messages to attract potential customers and set the company apart from its rivals. And HR teams play a key part in getting and keeping top talent, which is important for the growth of the company.

In today's very competitive market, companies have to do everything they can to stand out from the crowd and draw potential customers. This means that everyone in the company wants to sell, whether they have an official role in sales or not.

For example, customer service reps may need to help customers understand how valuable a product or service is and convince them to buy it. Marketing teams come up with messages and campaigns to help the company stand out from its competitors and draw new customers. And HR teams play a key part in getting and keeping top talent, which is important for the growth of the company.

Everyone in a business does something to help people and make the business successful. So, support needs to grow at an exponential rate to keep up with market needs and help companies stay competitive. This means giving workers the tools and help they need to work well with customers and other important people.

Distribution of Enablement
Roles in a Company

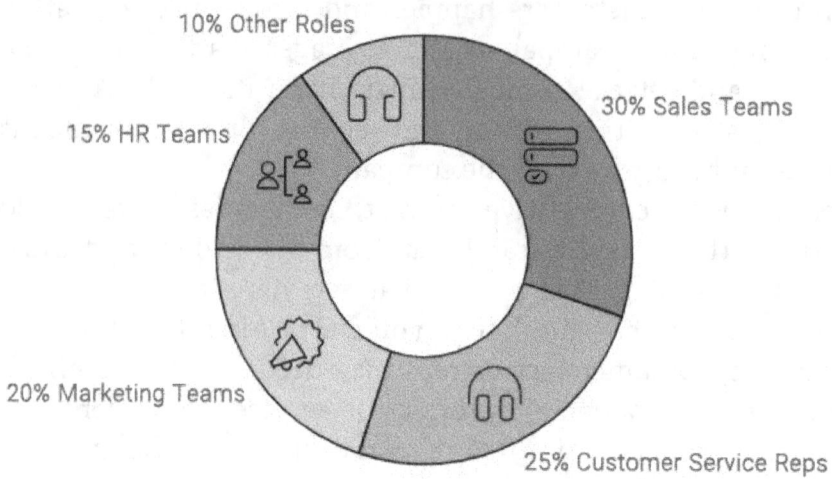

10% Other Roles

15% HR Teams

30% Sales Teams

20% Marketing Teams

25% Customer Service Reps

The Breakdown

To really grasp enablement, it is vital to split the practice into its basic pieces. Giving employees the information, skills, tools, and support they need to do their jobs well and add to the overall success of the business is what it means to enable them. This includes everything, from the first day of work and training to help and growth throughout an employee's job.

For a business to grow and meet its goals, it needs to have effective programs to help people do what they need to do. They can improve how well employees do their jobs, how much they get done, how happy customers are, and how well the business does generally. But for empowerment programs to work, they need to be well-planned, well-implemented, and well-supported. This takes a lot of time, money, and work, which is why many empowerment programs fail to bring about long-term change.

People are the first and perhaps most important part of enabling. For empowerment programs to work, they need to be planned, put into action, and backed by a team of skilled, committed people. These workers are different from the rest of the company because they have a unique set of skills, knowledge, and experience that sets them apart.

The Team

There are four main types of people who are needed for a support team to work well.

- The first is the thinker or visionary who understands enablement's needs and where it needs to go. This person is constantly innovating and challenging the status quo in order to deliver on the enablement promise.
- The second is the doer, or the implementer, who turns the vision into a reality. This individual is in charge of transforming ideas and concepts into practical, actionable plans and initiatives that can be implemented throughout the organization.

- The third type of influencer is the advocate, who works to build support and buy-in for enablement programs throughout the organization. This individual is adept at communicating the value of enablement to a diverse range of stakeholders, from senior leadership to front-line employees, and ensuring that everyone is on board with enablement initiatives.
- The fourth is the learner, or continuous improvement expert, who is constantly looking for ways to improve enablement programs and ensure that they meet the needs of the business and the employees. This individual is responsible for gathering feedback, analyzing data, and implementing changes to drive continuous improvement and success.

Support Team Roles

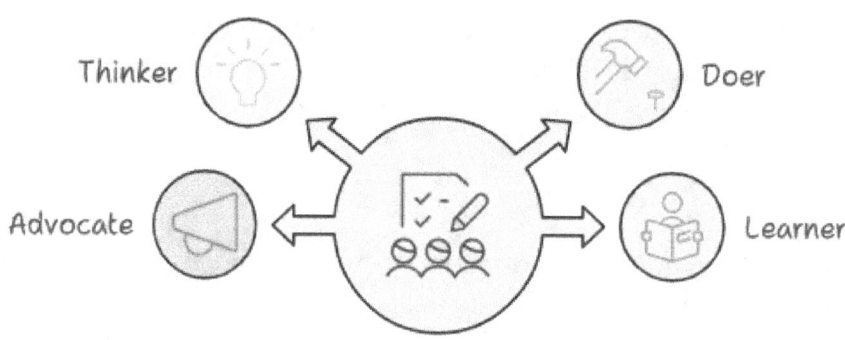

A good enablement team is built on these four categories of individuals. They are what makes empowerment programs work, and without them, the programs are doomed to fail.

If a team has the right people and a good mix of the four types of people listed above, it has a much better chance of making a real difference in the company. Each person brings a different set of skills and knowledge to the table. When these skills are joined and used well, the team can make big changes and improvements.

For example, the thinker gives the vision and direction for enablement programs, while the doer makes sure that the goal is turned into real, doable initiatives. The influencer gets organizational support and buy-in for the programs, while the learner works on ongoing growth and makes sure the programs meet the needs of the business and the workers.

This team can drive change and make a difference in ways that a single person or a team with a less balanced set of skills can't. When they work together and use each other's skills, they can make support programs that really work and lead to long-term success for the company.

Cross-functional teams

Cross-functional enablement teams are a great way for companies to help their workers and give them more power. People from different departments or roles make up these teams. They get together to work on enablement programs and projects. This can include sharing information, resources, and expertise, as well as helping and empowering each other through working together.

Leveraging Cross-Functional Enablement Teams for Organizational Success

Employees have access to a wide range of ideas and skills through cross-functional support teams. Employees have access to a wide range of ideas and skills through cross-functional support teams. This lets them look at problems and chances from different points of view, which leads to better and more creative solutions. Teams can also get a better understanding of their organization's goals and objectives by working together on support projects. This makes teams stronger and more effective.

- More collaboration and coordination: Cross-functional enablement teams can help break down walls and encourage more collaboration and coordination throughout the company. By bringing together people from different areas and roles, enablement teams can make it easier for people to share knowledge and resources. They can also help align and integrate enablement efforts across the company.
- Better customer experience and engagement: Cross-functional support teams can also help improve the experience and engagement of customers. By including workers from different departments in enablement efforts, companies can make sure that enablement programs are in line with customer wants and expectations. This makes enablement more complete and customer-focused.
- Better efficiency and effectiveness: Cross-functional enablement teams can also help improve the efficiency and effectiveness of enablement activities. By sharing resources and skills, enablement teams can use the organization's overall knowledge and experience to make enablement programs and projects that are more targeted, relevant, and successful.
- Better development and engagement of employees: Finally, cross-functional support teams can help improve the development and engagement of

employees. By getting workers involved in enablement efforts, companies can give them chances to learn, grow, and add to the success of the company. This can also help create a more interested and committed workforce.

The Structure

The next part of successful support is the methods of accomplishment. As the world has gotten faster and more digital, PowerPoint slideshows and live lessons have become less common. My method to enablement is to split it into four categories. Each category builds on the one before it to make a complete and effective program.

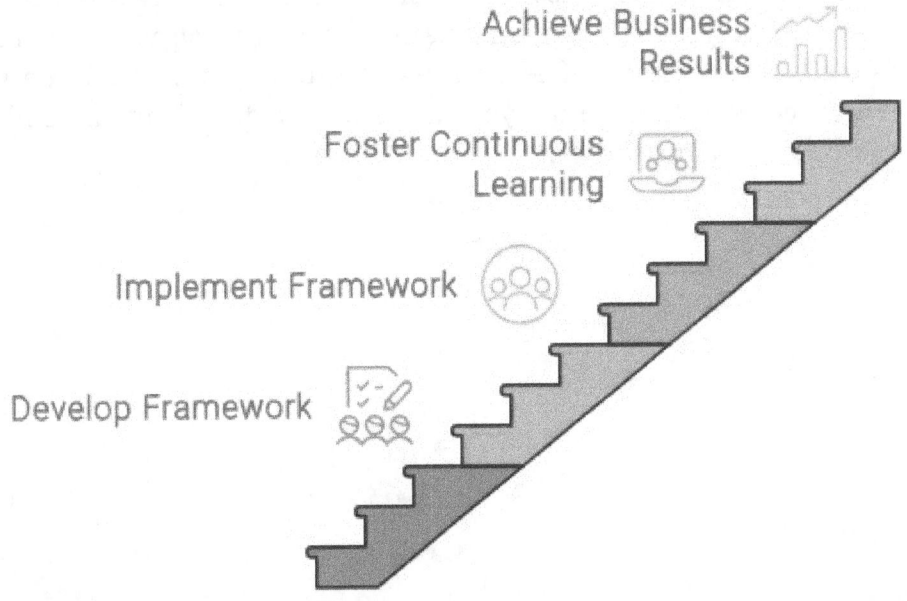

I Have build the following framework

Enablement Skill Stack Framework: Shaping Employee Growth through 4 Steps

This framework shows how important it is for businesses to keep learning and growing. By creating a learning culture, companies can keep their best employees, get their employees more involved, and get better business results. This support model creates a win-win situation for both the employees and the organization. The employees get the chance to grow and develop professionally, and the organization gets the skills and information that the employees have gained.

The value of this framework comes from its ability to help

workers keep learning and growing, which can lead to more job satisfaction and efficiency. Investing in the growth of their workers can make them more involved and motivated at work, which can lead to better business results. This framework also pushes businesses to put employee development at the top of their list of priorities and to create a place where people can learn and grow all the time.

My theory emphasizes how important it is for businesses to keep learning and growing. Organizations that use this support model can create a culture of learning and growth, keep their best employees, get their employees more involved, and, in the end, more for their customers.

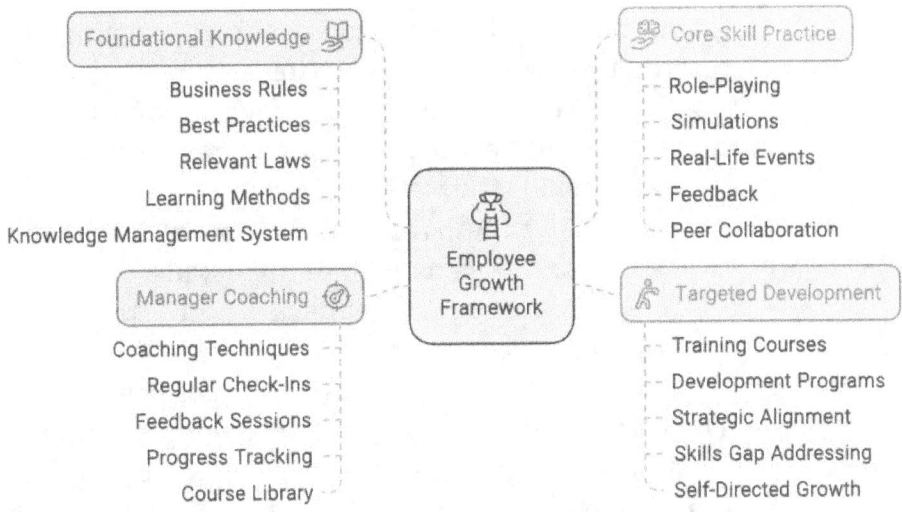

Based on the four steps listed, this is a framework for letting employees grow and improve:

- The first category is foundational knowledge,

Give your workers the knowledge they need to do their jobs well, such as business rules, best practices in the industry, and relevant laws. Provide different ways to learn, such as online training classes, webinars, workshops, and training on the job.

  - Give workers access to all important information related to their jobs, such as business rules, best practices in the industry, and relevant laws.
  - Provide different ways to learn, such as online training classes, webinars, workshops, and training on the job.
  - Set up a knowledge management system so that you can plan and share information well.

- The second category is core skill practice, let workers use role-playing, games, and real-life situations to practice the core skills they learned in step 1. Give them comments on how they're doing so they can improve their skills. Encourage comments and teamwork between peers to encourage learning and create a mindset of always getting better.

- Let workers use role-playing, simulations, and real-life events to practice the core skills they learned in step 1.
- Give them feedback on how well they did, so they can improve their skills.
- Encourage feedback and teamwork between peers to help people learn more and create a mindset of ongoing growth.

- The third category is targeted development, provide a list of training courses and development programs that workers can choose from based on their job, hobbies, and career goals. Make sure that the training programs are in line with the strategic goals of the business and that they fill in any skills gaps that were found in performance reviews. Encourage your workers to take charge of their own growth and give them the support and tools they need to do well.

- Give employees a list of training classes and development programs from which they can choose based on their job, their hobbies, and their future goals.
- Make sure that the training programs are in line with the strategic goals of the company and address any skills gaps found in performance reviews. • Encourage workers to take charge of their own growth and give them the support and tools they need to achieve.

- Manager coaching,

Managers should learn how to coach so they can help their team members reach their growth goals. Encourage regular check-ins and feedback meetings to see how things are going and figure out what needs to change. Encourage managers to tell workers to look back at the course list for more ways to learn and grow.

- Teach managers how to coach so they can help their team members reach their goals for growth.
- Encourage regular check-ins and feedback sessions to track progress and find places to improve. Encourage managers to point workers back to the course library for more training and development opportunities.

Managers must invest in the learning paths of their employees because it can be good for both the employees and the company as a whole. This includes teaching managers how to coach, giving them access to coaching tools, and giving them ongoing support and direction so that they can give their teams the help they need to succeed.

Managers should pay attention to:

Investing in workers' learning paths can help them improve their knowledge and skills, which can help them do a better job on the job. This can help drive the growth of a company and lead to better business results.

- Increasing employee involvement and motivation: Putting money into workers' learning paths shows them that the company cares about their growth and development. This can make them more interested and motivated, which can lead to better work and success.

- Keeping good employees: Investing in employees' learning paths can help keep good employees by giving them chances for growth and development. This can help keep people from leaving and save the company money and time that would have been spent on hiring and teaching new people.

◦ Making organizations more flexible and adaptable: Investing in the learning paths of workers can help them become more flexible and adaptable. Organizations can be better prepared to deal with changes and challenges in the business world if they give their workers the information and skills they need to do well in a variety of jobs and settings.

Continuous Enablement vs Event Enablement

C ontinuous enablement and event-based enablement are both good ways to give people and teams more power at work. They do have different goals and plans, though.

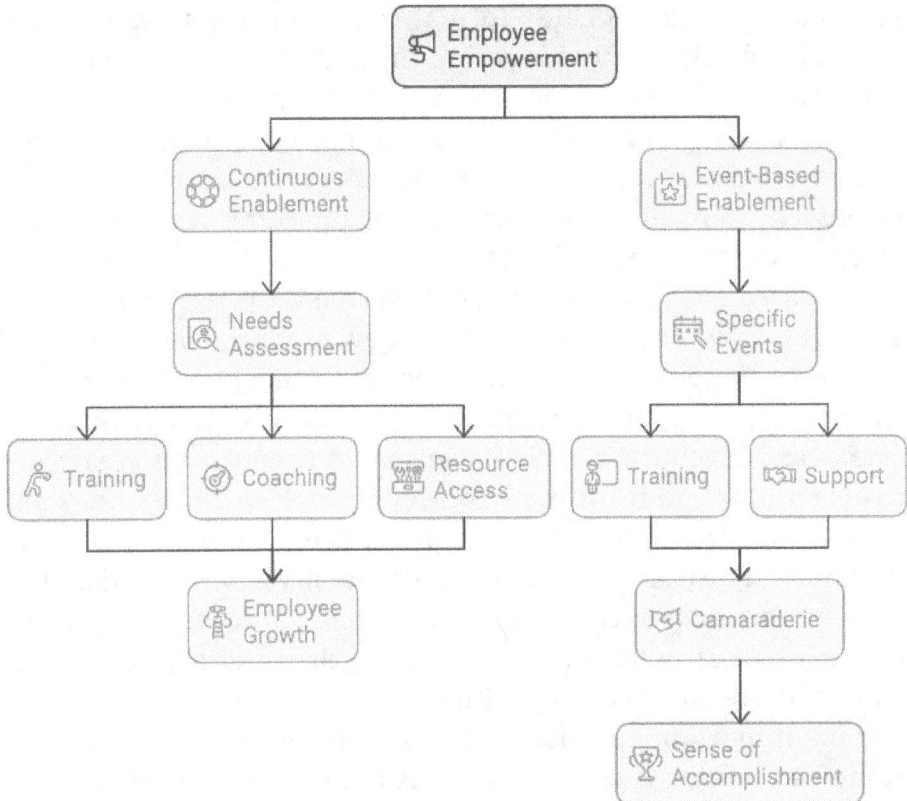

Continuous support is a key part of employee growth and the success of a company. Its main goal is to give people and teams the constant help and tools they need to do their jobs well. This includes giving them access to the tools and resources they need to do their jobs well, as well as giving them training, teaching, and mentoring.

The first step in the process of constant support is to figure out what a person or team needs. This evaluation can look at their current skills, knowledge, and abilities. It can also look for areas where they need to improve or where they may not have the tools they need. Once the review is done, a customized plan can be made to give them the right training, coaching, guidance, and access to the tools and resources they need to do their job well.

Through constant support, there are many ways to learn and get training. It can include formal training classes, training on the job, and self-directed learning through webinars, e-learning, and other tools. Coaching and tutoring can be done one-on-one, in small groups, or through online tools. Access to tools and resources can be given through on-site training or online resources. Tools and resources can be anything from software programs to specific equipment.

Event-based enablement, on the other hand, focuses on specific events or activities, like the start of a new product, company-wide efforts, or big projects. This method gives people and teams the training and support they need to successfully deal with these events and reach their goals. Event-based support is a great way to give people and teams more power at work. When workers get together for training and development events, they find a sense of camaraderie that makes their relationships stronger and makes it easier for them to talk to each other and work together. When they do well at certain events or tasks, they feel proud of their work and a sense of accomplishment.

But it's important to know that event-based support can have some bad effects. If training lessons are too close together or if people don't have a chance to practice what they've learned, they might not remember everything they've learned.

Even so, if event-based support is done right, it can make workers feel more loyal to the company. By putting money into the growth and success of people and teams, organizations show their dedication and give team members a feeling of investment and ownership.

Event-based enablement is a strong tool, but it's important to think about the possible downsides and make sure the training and support is repeated over time, just like a writer adds details to a story to keep readers interested and not lose them. This will make sure that both people and teams have the tools they need to do their best work and reach their goals.

Timing

Teaching employees everything at once is usually not a good idea because it can mean giving them a lot of information at once, which can be stressful and make it hard for them to remember and use. Most of the time, it's better to break up learning into smaller, more doable pieces and give workers chances to practice and use their new knowledge and skills over time.

"Enablement isn't just about giving salespeople content; it's also about giving them the right content at the right time to help them do their jobs well."

One of the main reasons why it doesn't work to teach everyone everything at once is that the brain isn't made to remember a lot of knowledge at once. When the brain is given a lot of information, it tends to filter out what it thinks is not important and only remember a small amount of what is given. This can make it hard for workers to remember what they've learned and use it in the real world.

Also, telling workers everything right away can make them less interested and less motivated. When employees are given too much information, they can feel overloaded and lose interest. This can make them less likely to want to learn and use what they have learned. By breaking learning down into smaller, more doable pieces, businesses can keep workers interested and driven while also making the learning experience more effective as a whole.

It's usually not a good idea to teach workers everything at once. By breaking up learning into smaller, more doable pieces, businesses can help employees remember and use what they've learned and get them more engaged and motivated. This will help people learn and grow in their jobs and help the group be more successful and have a bigger effect.

JITE is a way to learn and grow based on the idea that people are more likely to look for training and help when they have a specific problem or need to solve. This is like when people look up how to fix a broken washing machine on YouTube. In both cases, the person is looking for information and advice to help them solve a problem or meet a need.

The main difference between JITE and other ways of learning and growing is when and how the training is given. JITE training is given to employees right when they need it, instead of in a more general or formal way. This means that the training is more likely to be remembered and used because it is more related to the job.

Break it Down: The Power of Incremental Learning

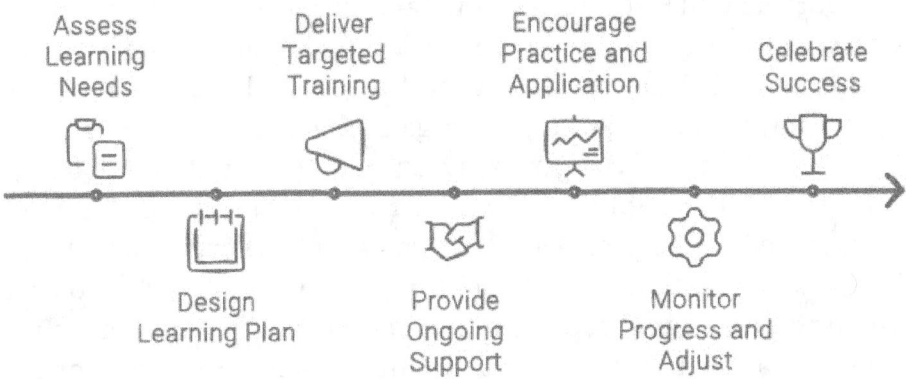

For example, if an employee is working on a job and runs into a problem they don't know how to solve, they can use a JITE tool to quickly and easily access a tutorial or guide that will help them understand and solve the problem. This saves the employee time and stress and makes it easier for them to do their job well and quickly.

Just-in-time enablement is a learning and development strategy that focuses on giving workers the information and skills they need right when they need them to improve speed and effectiveness.

Logistics

When it comes to performing enablement initiatives, logistics management is crucial. It's all about getting the right people in the right place at the right time with the right tools and resources. When all of these parts work together, the results will be better for both workers and the company. When things go well, everyone does well.

Think about it, for example, when planning a training event. If the right people aren't there or if they don't have the right tools, the teaching might not be as good as it could be. But when everything is in place, things are very different. The training will go well, and the workers will learn and remember more.

Costs and risks can also be cut down with the help of logistics management. Unexpected expenditures and delays may be avoided by proper planning and organizing logistics. For example, if you're planning a training event but haven't thought about how to get the supplies there, you might have to pay for an unexpected delivery or even have to cancel the event. But if you have transportation management in place, you will have thought about these things ahead of time and everything will go smoothly.

To summarize, logistics management is an essential component of successful enablement efforts. It all comes down to getting the right people, with the right tools and resources, to the right place at the right time. When this happens, everybody wins!

Instructional Design

Effective instructional design plays a crucial role in enablement by ensuring that learning and development activities are both engaging and productive. Instructional design involves creating learning materials and experiences in a way that aids retention and comprehension. This necessitates aligning the information, materials, and activities with the training's goals and objectives while considering the audience's needs, preferences, and learning styles.

This approach enhances the effectiveness and relevance of employee training and support. By thoughtfully crafting learning experiences, enablement professionals can produce materials and activities that are engaging, practical, and pertinent, leading to improved learning outcomes and job performance.

Furthermore, robust instructional design can contribute to more efficient and cost-effective learning and development efforts. Enablement practitioners can avoid wasting time and resources on ineffective materials and activities by ensuring they align closely with the training's goals and objectives. This strategy maximizes the impact of training and support while conserving time and money. For instance, if a company aims to train employees on new software, an instructional designer would create materials and activities that align with the training's goals while addressing the audience's needs, preferences, and learning styles. This results in more engaging and useful training, enhancing learning and job performance.

High-quality instructional design not only makes training more successful but also more efficient and economical. By ensuring materials and activities align well with the training's goals and objectives, enablement professionals can minimize wasted resources and maximize the effectiveness of training and support.

Breaking Down Barriers and Silos

To truly empower people, we must dismantle barriers and silos. This chapter discusses overcoming common obstacles to enablement, such as organizational structure, cultural behaviors, and resource limitations. Here are some usual barriers to enabling and ways to overcome them:

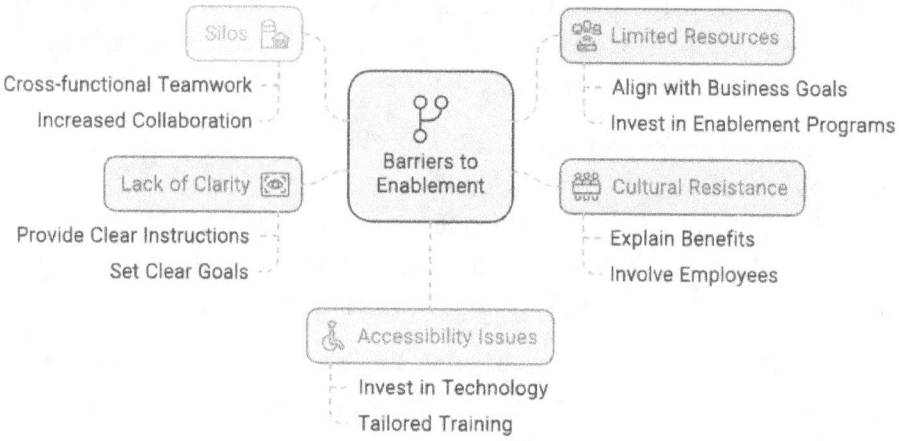

Silos

One of the biggest things that gets in the way of support is the fact that many companies work in separate silos. Most of the time, departments and teams work on their own, with little or no contact or collaboration with other parts of the company. To break down silos, there needs to be more cross-functional teamwork and contact. Organizations can make better use of the skills and knowledge of their workers if they break down silos and encourage a more creative atmosphere.

Limited Resources

A lack of resources can be a major hurdle to enabling. For support programs to work, they need time, money, and technology. Organizations must be willing to spend in enablement programs if they want to give their workers the tools and resources they need to do well. Also, for the best use of resources, it's important to make sure that support programs are in line with business goals.

Cultural Resistance

It can be hard to get past cultural norms and reluctance to change. For support programs to work, both leaders and workers need to be on board. To get past cultural reluctance, it is important to explain the benefits of support and get employees involved in the process. A mindset of continuous learning and change can be created in an organization by giving people a sense of ownership and getting them involved.

Lack of Clarity

Uncertainty about jobs, responsibilities, and methods can be a big problem for enabling. To do well, workers need clear instructions and goals. Through enablement programs, employees must be given the information and tools they need to understand their jobs, tasks, and goals. This means giving clear information about the organization's purpose, beliefs, and goals.

Accessibility Issues

Accessibility problems can make it hard to help people. Enablement programs must be available to all workers, no matter where they work, what their job is, or what technology they use. This means that the company needs to spend money on technology that lets workers learn from home and on training that fits their needs and the way they learn.

Lack of Leadership Support

To be effective, enablement programs need the backing of leaders. If leaders aren't fully behind the program, employees might not take it seriously, and the program might not reach its goals.

Poor Communication

Communication is an important part of enabling, but it can also get in the way. If communication is unclear or inconsistent, it may be hard for employees to understand their jobs or goals, which can cause confusion and anger.

Outdated Training Methods

Traditional methods of training, like talks or slide shows, may not work for all workers. Organizations need to find new ways to train their workers in ways that are interesting, involved, and specific to their needs.

Employee Resistance to Technology

Some employees may not want to use technology, which can hurt the success of programs that use digital tools to help people do their jobs better. For workers to feel comfortable with new tools, organizations must give them the right training and help.

Inadequate Accountability

Enablement initiatives must be held accountable for their outcomes. If there are no measurements or ways to track progress, it may be hard to tell if the program is meeting its goals. Organizations need to set up clear measures and measure the program's success on a regular basis to make sure it is having a positive effect.

CHAPTER 4

Enablement supporting new HR trends

What is quiet hiring? What implications does this have for Enablement and its role in the phenomenon?

Quiet hiring is a method of identifying and rewarding "high-flyers" within an organisation. This can be manifested through bonuses, promotions, salary increases, and assignments to more challenging tasks. The premise is that these employees, by exceeding their standard duties, will contribute more significantly to the company. Research indicates that high achievers can be up to 400% more effective than average employees, making it beneficial to recognise and reward their contributions. However, not all employees fall into the high-flyer category. Thus, it is essential to find ways to assist and engage all employees to ensure the overall success of the company.

Enablement can provide a robust foundation for developing a quiet hiring strategy.

Enablement might be a highly effective approach for identifying and supporting high-performing individuals ready to exceed expectations in their roles. By offering training and support, companies can enhance their sales representatives' skills and identify those with the highest potential. Providing the appropriate tools and resources can further aid high achievers in becoming more productive and successful in their positions.

A significant advantage of this method is enhancing employees' flexibility in their roles. By delivering continuous training and support, companies enable their workforce to acquire new skills and take on additional responsibilities. This adaptability is critical in today's rapidly changing business environment where employees must be prepared to handle evolving challenges.

Various support mechanisms can facilitate this process, including virtual meetings, learning tools, social learning, virtual and augmented reality, and AI-based learning. These methods equip employees with the necessary knowledge and skills to perform their jobs effectively while allowing them to learn at their own pace and in a manner that suits them best. Implementing these enablement strategies can foster a culture of continuous learning and growth, motivating high achievers.

According to Dr. Ruth Gotian's article on Forbes titled "How to Find, Keep, and Lead High Achievers,"

High-achieving employees can be among the most effective but also the most challenging to retain. While better pay may attract them elsewhere, the absence of mentorship or clarity on career advancement can also be contributing factors. Despite their potential to be 400% more productive than the average worker, these employees often receive less attention and support compared to those struggling to meet goals. Many organisations lack formal mechanisms to identify and cultivate high achievers into future leaders, resulting in discontent and stagnation.

This could lead to losing talented employees and hiring individuals who underperform. Research indicates that providing value to high achievers can increase productivity more effectively than offering bonuses or salary raises. To retain and develop high-achievers, organisations should invest in their professional development by creating opportunities for innovation, curiosity, and raising performance standards.

Assigning greater responsibility to high-performing employees can help retain and motivate them. One approach is to offer them ongoing projects and tasks that challenge them and provide opportunities to collaborate with top leaders and different teams.

For instance, allowing them to lead task forces, cross-functional teams, or devise solutions to organisational issues. Giving them a platform to present their ideas to senior leadership can earn them respect and a voice in decision-making processes.

Assigning them areas of responsibility akin to CEO duties can also inspire and engage these employees. When making decisions affecting high achievers that are outside their direct responsibilities, it's crucial to provide comprehensive context and maintain transparency. Treating them as decision-makers rather than mere order-takers fosters empowerment and respect, which are key to retaining and motivating high-performing workers.

Enablement Methods

Digital mediums changed the delivery of enablement, enabling new and interesting methods to engage people and assist their learning and development. Some of the most important ways that digital media are used to allow are:

Virtual sessions

Modern enablement includes virtual sessions and workshops, which give employees the freedom and ease they need to access training and development programs from anywhere, at any time. On the other hand, the Covid-19 pandemic has led to a widespread problem called "virtual fatigue," in which many people feel tired and stressed by the number of virtual meetings and sessions they have to attend.

To solve this problem, the internet meetings and workshops that are part of enablement programs need to include new and different parts. Some ways to do this are to include games and other interactive elements, to use themes and other visual tools to make the meetings more interesting, and to give regular breaks and socializing opportunities.

By making virtual meetings and workshops more creative and interesting, enablement programs can help workers get over "virtual fatigue" and have a better, more enjoyable time learning. This will help make the empowerment program and the company as a whole more successful and get more people involved.

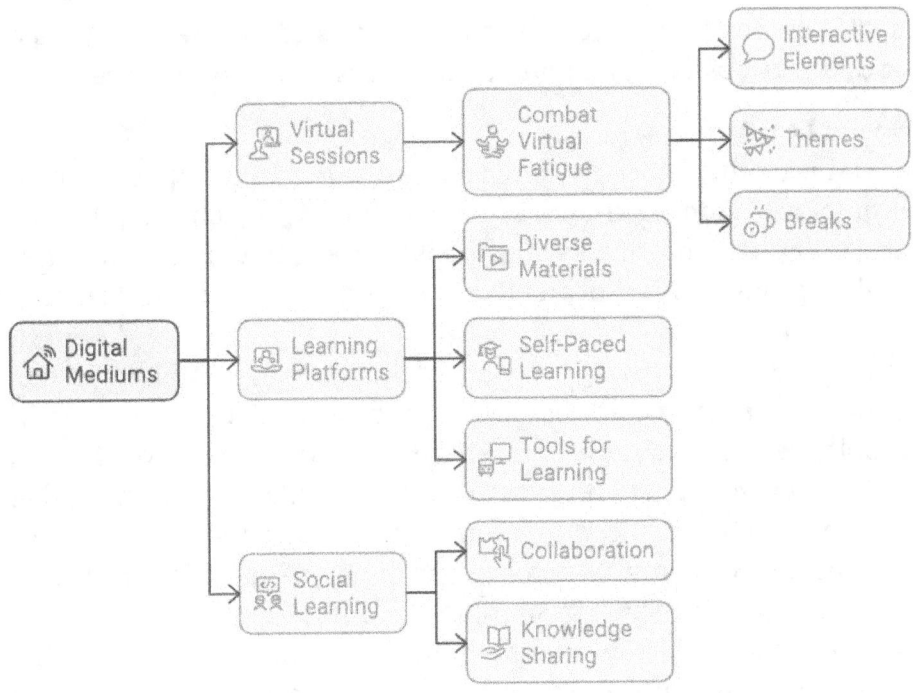

Learning Platforms

Online learning tools are an important part of modern support because they give workers access to a wide range of learning materials and resources. Most of the time, these sites offer a lot of different kinds of material, like movies, podcasts, interactive modules, and other types of media.

One of the best things about online learning tools is that workers can learn at their own pace and when it's most convenient for them. This means that workers don't have to stick to a strict plan of classes and workshops. Instead, they can access the learning materials whenever it's best for them. This makes learning easier to get to and more practical, and it could get more employees involved and interested.

Not only do many online learning platforms give you access to learning materials, but they also have tools and features that help you learn. For example, many platforms have recording and reporting tools that allow managers and trainers to keep track of the progress of each employee and give them specific feedback and help. This can help make sure that workers get the help they need to do their jobs well and help the business as a whole succeed.

Social Learning

Social learning is a fairly new idea in the world of support, but it is quickly becoming known as a powerful way to help people learn and grow. The goal of this method is to use social media and other online groups to build a collaborative and interesting learning environment.

One of the best things about social learning is that it lets employees share what they know and how good they are at it. Employees, for example, can share the best ways to do things, talk about problems and how to solve them, and help and guide each other. This can create a sense of community and teamwork within the company, which can make people more interested in and willing to take part in support programs.

Social learning lets workers share their knowledge and skills and work together on projects and other learning activities. For example, employees can work together on case studies, exercises, and other ways to learn together. This can help people learn how to solve problems, think critically, and build other important skills needed for success in the modern workplace.

Social learning is also the process by which people in their social surroundings watch and copy the actions of other people. People think that this kind of learning is important for developing complicated behaviors and skills as well as traditional practices and norms.

Social learning has the ability to be a big part of how people learn and get new skills in the future of support. This is because social learning lets people learn and get better at things by watching and imitating rather than by being told directly or making mistakes. People can learn from the mistakes and wins of others, which makes learning faster and better.

But there are limits to social learning in this way. People, for example, may not always be able to find people who can show them how to act and learn skills they want to learn. Also, biases and social norms can affect social learning, making it hard for people to see and learn a wide range of behaviors and skills.

Overall, social learning is a key part of human growth that has the potential to make a big difference in how well people can learn and build new skills. But it's important to know what its limits are and think of ways to get around them if you want to use it to help people reach their full potential.

Execution

Divide your content into chunks.

Divide your learning content into smaller, easier-to-handle "chunks" to keep your students from being overwhelmed by a lot of knowledge. This method, called "chunking," helps learners stay interested and motivated by letting them focus on one idea or part of a topic at a time. For example, if you're making training on how to better communicate with customers, you might not want to put all five skills into one long module. Instead, you might want to break it up into smaller modules that help learners to build their general skill set gradually. This could include movies, real-world examples, information checks, and a final test, all of which focus on a certain part of communicating with customers. By breaking up your content in this way, it will be easier for people to understand and remember. Divide your learning content into smaller, easier-to-handle "chunks" to keep your students from being overwhelmed by a lot of knowledge. This method, called "chunking," helps learners stay interested and motivated by letting them focus on one idea or part of a topic at a time. For example, if you're making training on how to better communicate with customers, you might not want to put all five skills into one long module. Instead, you might want to break it up into smaller modules that help learners to build their general skill set gradually. This could include movies, real-world examples, information checks, and a final test, all of which focus on a certain part of communicating with customers. By breaking up your content in this way, it will be easier for people to understand and remember.

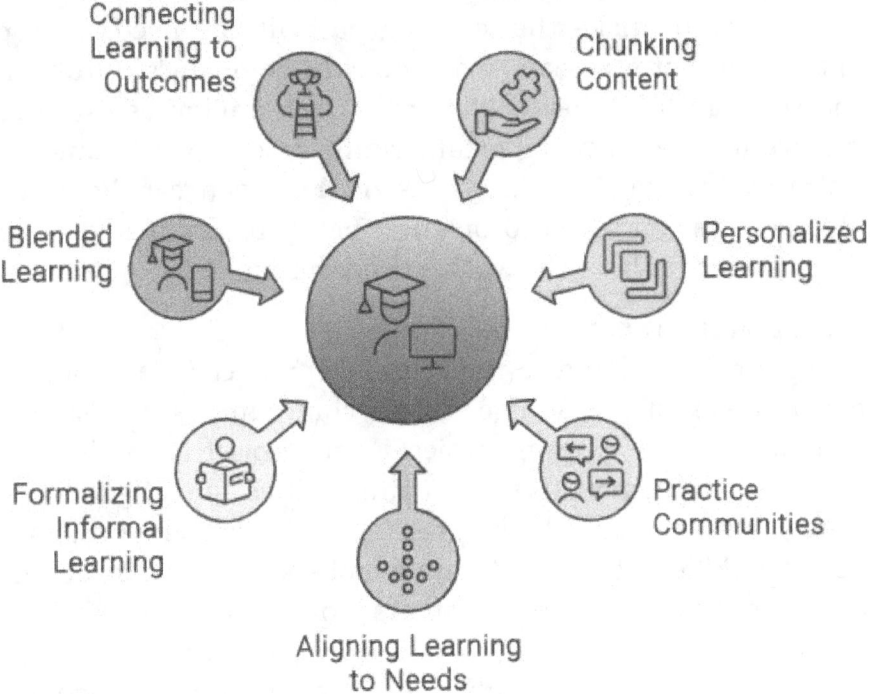

Strategies for Effective Learning and Development

Connecting Learning to Outcomes

Chunking Content

Blended Learning

Personalized Learning

Formalizing Informal Learning

Practice Communities

Aligning Learning to Needs

Allow for personalized learning paths.
Instead of making everyone go through the same training, it is often better to make the learning path fit the needs of each person. Long-term workers who know the company's culture and processes can learn new skills faster, and employees can focus on learning the most important skills instead of training that is already known. By taking this method, you can help your employees get up to speed on their new jobs faster and better, which is good for both the workers and the business.

Create practice communities.
It is important to build communities of practice focused around specific areas of knowledge. These communities can support transformational learning projects and project-based learning across the company. If these communities are aligned with strategic needs like Marketing, Learning, HR, and Finance, and if they have skilled leaders and team members to back them up, they can be very helpful to the business. For instance, an Assistant Controller might be in charge of a Finance Community of Practice, which might have team members who are experts in payments, IT, accounting, accounts payable, and accounts receivable.

Align learning to needs rather than wants
Business stakeholders tend to see learning as a means to an end. They prefer known methods that can improve performance or knowledge. As a learning worker, it's important to figure out why performance or knowledge problems are happening and suggest the best way to fix them, even if it's not what the client asked for at first. When you understand the theory and principles of adult learning, you can make solutions fit the unique needs of the student. For example, if the goal is to build teamwork and boost morale, a hands-on action learning practice may be more motivating than a standard classroom lesson on how to deal with coworkers.

Make your informal learning more formal.

Organizations that use a growth mindset concept usually encourage long-term employees to take ownership of their professional development and explore self-directed learning. This method works best for adults who want to learn because it gives them the freedom to choose the kinds of learning tasks that are most interesting and important to them. Self-directed learning can be helped by giving people access to videos, papers, and interactive classes, among other things, that they can use to learn on their own. A learning management system (LMS) can store these materials so that they are easy to find and progress can be tracked. If your group doesn't already have an LMS, you might want to think about getting one to make it easier to help people learn on their own.

Build a blended learning solution

Think about combining learning situations to get your students interested and make learning more fun and involved for them. This could be done by mixing in-person classes with online courses or by using writing tools to make your own online courses. These tools can help you make dynamic and interesting learning materials by letting you make slide-based classes with quizzes, conversation simulations, screencasts, and other interactive elements.

Connect learning to expected outcomes.

Do most of your employees learn through eLearning or instructor-led training classes, which are then tested? How well has this method helped your kids meet their wants and reach their goals?

Many employee learning programs teach a wide range of skills, information, processes, and routines, as well as things like safety, orientation, and onboarding. To choose the best method for your learning program, think about the performance goals you want your workers to reach and use what you know about how adults learn to choose a method that fits with these goals.

For example, think about a new person hired to work in customer service. They might need to be able to deal with customer disputes and solve problems quickly and well. An experiential learning method, such as role-playing or simulated customer contacts in a training setting, could let trainees practice and apply their customer service skills in a realistic way, preparing them to handle real-life situations on the job.

Virtual and Augmented Reality

Virtual and augmented reality (VR and AR) are being utilized more and more in enabling to provide immersive and engaging learning experiences. For example, virtual reality and augmented reality can be used to create training models and situations that let workers practice their skills in a safe and controlled environment. One of the main benefits of using VR and AR in enablement is that it lets workers experience real-world-like situations that are both interesting and accurate. Employees can practice their skills in a safe, controlled setting, so there is no need for expensive training activities or simulations that take a lot of time and money.

VR and AR can be used to make unique learning experiences that are based on the needs and skills of each employee, as well as to make learning more fun. For example, VR and AR can be used to create personalized situations and simulations that challenge and interest each employee while also giving them the help and feedback they need to improve their skills and performance.

Virtual reality (VR) and augmented reality (AR) activation costs can change based on a number of factors, such as the type of technology used and the application or training program that is being put in place. But in general, the cost of using VR and AR for enablement is likely to be higher than the cost of using standard methods like in-person teaching or printed materials.

One reason for this is that VR and AR technologies often require buying and maintaining special tools, like VR headsets or AR glasses. Also, making and using VR and AR training programs can take a lot of time and money, especially if you need to hire specialized staff or experts from outside the company.

On the other hand, the higher cost may be worth it if the benefits of using VR and AR for support are worth it. For example, VR and AR technology can make learning more intense and interesting, which makes training more effective and efficient. Also, VR and AR can be used to make learning settings that are lifelike and active in ways that would be hard or impossible to do with traditional methods. On the other hand, the higher cost may be worth it if the benefits of using VR and AR for support are worth it. For example, VR and AR technology can make learning more intense and interesting, which makes training more effective and efficient. Also, VR and AR can be used to make learning spaces that are lifelike and active.

Artificial Intelligence

Next up is AI, which, in my opinion, is where the future of enabling rests.

AI can be used to handle business processes in a number of ways. One way is through natural language processing (NLP) techniques. These algorithms can be taught to recognize human speech and pull the useful information from text-based data like emails and papers. This can be used to automate jobs like data entry, which saves companies time and makes them less likely to make mistakes.

AI can help people make decisions by giving them ideas and suggestions based on facts. For example, a company's sales data could be used to train an AI system to find trends and patterns. The AI system could then make suggestions about how to change the focus of sales training to match with sales. This can help businesses make better choices and keep up with the competition in their market.

AI can be used to improve the experience of employees by giving them more personalized interactions and services. It can also be used to improve business processes and the way decisions are made. For example, a chatbot that is driven by AI could be used 24 hours a day to answer workers' questions right away. This could make employees happier and help companies build stronger ties with their customers at the same time.

The use of AI in corporate support is expected to help companies become more productive, customer-focused, and efficient. AI can help companies improve their operations and better serve their customers by eliminating boring and time-consuming chores, giving insights and suggestions based on data, and making the customer experience better.

Digital media are giving us new and exciting ways to support staff learning and growth and help with enabling. By using these platforms, businesses can make more interesting and successful enablement programs that have a real impact and lead to success.

CHAPTER 5

Content Management

"Enablement is not just about providing content. It's about providing the right content to the right person at the right time to help them be successful."

The availability of content is crucial for enablement because it ensures employees can access the information, skills, and resources they need to succeed in their roles. By providing relevant and accurate information, companies can support employees' learning and development, enhance their performance, and help them achieve their goals.

Furthermore, granting employees access to these materials can improve their overall job satisfaction and engagement. Employees are more likely to feel supported and valued by their employer when they have the necessary tools and information to perform their tasks efficiently, which can boost their motivation and dedication.

There is a close relationship between enablement and content management due to the critical role that content plays in enablement. Individuals and teams are considered enabled when they possess the knowledge, skills, and resources required for success. This often includes access to various types of content such as training materials, documents, videos, and other resources.

Conversely, content management involves organizing, storing, and managing this material so that it is easily accessible to those who need it. Examples include setting up a centralized content repository, implementing classification and tagging systems, and maintaining current and accurate content.

By effectively managing the content used in the enablement process, organizations can make their programs more effective by ensuring that employees have the right resources at the right time. Efficient content management also helps organizations save time and money by avoiding duplicate content creation and ensuring optimal use. Maintaining the essential, intertwined relationship between enablement and content management is vital for fostering individual and team success in the workplace.

CHAPTER 6

Reach People Through Games

Can games benefit a business?

Absolutely, games can be advantageous for businesses. Gamification, which involves incorporating game design elements into non-game scenarios, can be highly effective. By integrating aspects like points, badges, and leaderboards into business processes and training sessions, employers can boost employee engagement and motivation. This can result in increased productivity and performance.

Simulation games offer another way to support businesses. Such games can train employees in various business procedures and scenarios, allowing them to refine their skills within a secure, controlled environment. This is particularly beneficial for complex or hazardous tasks, as it enables learning and error correction without real-world consequences.

Additionally, gamified learning tools are excellent for business use. By incorporating rewards and game-like challenges, these platforms maintain employee interest and motivation while they acquire new skills and knowledge. This approach can enhance the enjoyment and efficiency of training, leading to better retention and job performance.

"Using Minecraft to Educate and Engage Employees in a Virtual Sales Launch"

During the COVID-19 pandemic in 2020, our company had to pivot to a virtual sales launch, which was challenging. We aimed to create an engaging and informative event that did not require prolonged computer screen time. Being an avid Minecraft fan, I saw an opportunity to utilize the game's platform to create a virtual representation of our new business processes.

We collaborated with game designers and industry experts to develop a Minecraft world that was both entertaining and educational. The finished product allowed participants to navigate this virtual world, completing quests for a grand prize. We also recorded game footage and presented it during the event.

Implementation: We invited all employees, including many of their family members and children, to join the Minecraft event.

Results: The Minecraft event was hugely successful, with numerous employees finding it both enjoyable and instructive. The initiative positively influenced morale; months later, employees continued to reference the game in daily conversations, indicating its efficacy in communicating new business procedures.

This case study highlights the potential of video games to engage employees and provide educational value in a virtual format. Our workforce appreciated the Minecraft game, which enhanced their comprehension of new business practices. We recommend leveraging video games as a dynamic and interactive teaching tool, even in remote work scenarios.

The following year, our organization faced the challenge of educating 800 employees about their roles and the functioning of the organization. Whereas previous years relied on face-to-face meetings, the pandemic required a switch to virtual learning. When we resumed in-person interactions the next year, we developed a board game to facilitate learning and engagement.

"How a Large Company Can Use a Board Game to Improve Organizational Understanding"

Method: Collaborating with learning and development specialists alongside subject matter experts, we created the board game using design thinking principles, such as research and prototyping, to ensure it was both engaging and informative. The final product was a tangible board game with components and rules for each segment.

Implementation: We facilitated the board game sessions with groups of 20 employees at a time, led by a supervisor who managed the game flow and answered questions. Multiple sessions were organized over several weeks to accommodate everyone.

The board game was tremendously successful, involving close to 800 participants. Feedback was overwhelmingly positive, with employees finding the game both fun and educational. Post-game surveys revealed that the board game significantly improved understanding of individual roles and organizational operations.

This case study demonstrates that game-based learning can effectively educate large groups about organizational functions. Employees received the board game well, gaining better insights into the company's workings. We endorse game-based learning as an engaging and interactive method for employee education and involvement.

In the end, gaming can be a useful tool for corporate enablement because it can help companies motivate and engage workers, improve their skills and knowledge, and eventually drive better business results.

CHAPTER 7

Mindsets

Mindsets play a crucial role in the success of support programs, as individuals within a company possess varying levels of knowledge, experience, and skills. To maximize empowerment, it is essential to elevate everyone to the same level by providing appropriate guidance and support.

My strategy for addressing this challenge involves designing programs that encourage individuals to step outside their comfort zones and begin from a common baseline. This can be achieved through various methods, including games, activities, and scenarios that foster innovative thinking and skill acquisition.

After completing these exercises, participants can return to their roles and discuss their newfound insights. This approach ensures that key lessons are retained and applied in real-world contexts.

Overall, my approach to empowerment revolves around equipping individuals with the necessary tools, resources, and opportunities to succeed. By creating engaging and impactful enablement programs, businesses can drive growth and success while fostering the development and prosperity of their employees.

Enablement Pitfalls

Loss of Focus

In enablement, one of the most common mistakes companies make is to lose sight of their customers. When making a sales training plan, you should think about the people who will actually use it: the sales reps who work directly with customers.

Research shows that three-quarters of enablement leaders think that the seller's experience is important for effective enablement programs, but many continue to focus on deliverables or business goods instead of the reps themselves. As a sales enabler, you need to know what your sales reps' ongoing needs and challenges are and give them the help and tools they need in the right manner and at the right time. Even though the enablement plan should be in line with the company's general goals, the main goal is to give the sales team the tools they need to bring in more money.

To make enablement more successful, think about the customer and find out what the salespeople who work with them need. When businesses know this, they can better focus the resources they need to help their sales team succeed.

Rinse & Repeat

One of the most common mistakes businesses make when it comes to enablement is repeating the same ideas and methods year after year without examining if they are still relevant or successful.

When you do the same thing year after year, you can get stuck and stop making progress. The business world is always changing, and what worked in the past might not work as well now. Organizations need to be able to change and respond to these changes if they want to keep being successful.

Also, workers' needs and standards change over time, so companies need to keep track of what their employees need to be successful and give it to them. By doing this, businesses can make sure that their support strategies match the current needs of their workers and the state of the business.

If you use the same support tactics year after year, your employees may lose interest and stop being as motivated. If employees don't feel like they are being pushed or given the chance to grow, they may lose interest and motivation. This can hurt their performance and the success of the company.

Organizations need to look at and change their support plans on a regular basis to make sure they match the needs of their workers and the state of the business. By not doing the same thing year after year, organizations can give their workers the tools they need to reach their full potential and help the company as a whole succeed.

Generational change

The workforce is changing, which brings new obstacles and chances to help people. When it comes to enabling, the younger workers have different needs and expectations, and companies must change their tactics to meet these needs.

The way people think is one of the biggest differences between younger and older people. Younger workers are more likely to be self-motivated and take initiative. They also tend to think more like entrepreneurs. They like to make their own decisions and have a lot of freedom, and they are less likely to respond to standard, top-down methods to enabling.

To successfully enable the younger workforce, organizations must take a more bottom-up method. This means giving workers the tools and freedom they need to be in charge of their own growth and development. Some examples of this are self-directed learning chances, mentoring and coaching programs, and flexible work plans.

Technology is another important way to help young people get jobs. Younger workers are more likely to know how to use technology and to use it in their daily lives. Organizations should use technology to make digital training programs that are both easy to use and fun for younger workers. This is shown by things like online training, virtual guidance, and digital tools that help with self-directed learning.

Younger workers often value having a good mix between work

and life, and companies should keep this in mind when making enablement programs. Flexible work hours and the ability to work from home are becoming more and more important for younger workers.

Younger workers have different needs and expectations, so businesses have to change their plans to meet these needs. For the younger workers to be able to do their jobs well, it's important to use a bottom-up method, use technology, and give them freedom and a good work-life balance.

Content

Sales is an area that changes all the time, so it's important for companies to keep their enablement materials up-to-date. Old content can become out of date and useless, and using it can cost you deals and make you look poor to prospects. For example, a tech company that offers a business software tool. They have a set of enablement tools, like a white paper that explains the software's features and benefits and a sales script that reps use to pitch the product to potential buyers.

For the past two years, these tools have been used successfully to close deals. On the other hand, the company has just put out a new version of the software with new features and improvements. The white paper and sales script don't properly describe the product as it is now, which could cause misunderstanding or pushback from customers.

To avoid this, groups should check their content regularly and change it as needed. This makes sure that sales reps have access to up-to-date and correct information, which is important for closing deals and keeping a professional image. Also, businesses should make sure that the material for enablement is easy to find so that reps can quickly find the information they need to answer prospects' questions well.

Lack Informal Enablement

Formal enablement, like training classes, lessons, and handbooks, can give sales reps useful information and skills, but it's not enough to set them up for success on their own. Informal enablement, which includes less organized learning chances like peer learning, teaching, mentoring, and sharing lessons learned, is also important for sales growth and success.

Formal support is good for hiring and developing leaders, but it doesn't give reps the soft skills and complicated strategies they need to do well in their jobs. Informal enablement allows for more personalized and ongoing learning, which helps sales reps learn how to sell better than official tools can. To fully back your sales team and help them succeed, you need to give them both formal and informal ways to learn. This gives reps the information and skills they need to do their jobs well, as well as the chance to keep learning and growing.

Out of Sync Teams

Both the sales and marketing teams are important to a company's ability to make money, but they often don't work together. To make a good sales training plan, it's important for these teams to work together and coordinate their efforts.

The sales team is in charge of finishing deals and turning leads into customers. The marketing team is in charge of making and sharing content to attract and engage potential customers. Both teams need to work together to make sure that their messages are clear and that their goals are the same.

When the marketing and sales teams don't talk to each other, leads and customers may get different messages. This can lead to confusion and lack of trust, which makes it hard for the sales team to close deals. When the marketing and sales teams work together and coordinate their efforts, they can make a plan that works well and brings in sales.

Failure to Encourage and Integrate Feedback

Gathering feedback from your sales staff on a regular basis is crucial to good enablement. The whole point of enablement strategies is to help and encourage your salespeople, and their feedback is essential to making sure these strategies work and are useful.

If you don't get feedback, your support tools could become outdated and useless. The market and sales reps' needs are always changing, so it's important to stay on top of these changes and adjust. It is important to not only listen to feedback but also do something about it. Adding feedback to your support plan can make it work better and help you solve any problems that might come up. Whether the feedback is about a big problem or a small change, it is important to think about it and make the changes that are needed.

A good enablement plan needs regular feedback from your sales team. By asking for and acting on feedback, organizations can make sure that their training tools are always useful, up-to-date, and suited to the needs of their sales teams.

Vague Accountabilities

True, enablement teams are typically tugged in several directions by stakeholders with diverse expectations, such as business development, marketing, and sales managers. and that's before we get to the top level of management. This can cause problems for your team and make them feel uncomfortable about who they work for and what parts of their work they are responsible for: A Harris Interactive study found that unclear work standards are one of the top five things that cause stress at work. You can take charge of this by calling out to your partners, including your own team members, to remind them of your team's goals and ask for their help. Create and share a plan for working with other groups, including how to make the first contact. This could be informal, like asking them to email you first, or more formal, like using a Trello board and setting up regular meetings. This can, of course, be changed as your team grows. Sales support is all about being able to change.

CHAPTER 8

Measurement

A ccording to the enablement collective, 73.3% of enablers rank win/close rate as one of the top three significant indicators for evaluating salespeople.

Companies can assess empowerment in various ways, depending on the program's goals and objectives. Popular methods include measuring participation and interaction to gauge the effectiveness and success of enablement programs. Tracking the number of employees attending enablement classes and training provides insights into their interest and engagement, helping identify areas with high interest and potential gaps or issues.

Additionally, monitoring the level of communication and engagement during enablement meetings offers valuable information about the program's effectiveness. For instance, if many participants sign up but do not interact or engage, it may indicate that the program isn't meeting their needs or interests. By tracking these metrics, businesses can make adjustments to enhance their training programs' engagement and efficacy.

Measuring knowledge and skill acquisition is another crucial way to determine the effectiveness of support programs. Pre- and post-tests help businesses understand how much information and skills participants have gained, shedding light on the program's success and identifying areas needing further assistance or training.

Performance growth is a key metric to understand the impact

of enablement programs on business results. Tracking the sales and revenue achievements of employees who have completed the training provides valuable insights into the program's effect on the company's bottom line. Comparing the performance of trained employees with those who did not participate offers a deeper understanding of enablement's value and impact.

Various methods exist to measure the success of support programs, chosen based on the program's specific goals and objectives. By tracking these metrics, businesses gain useful insights into their enablement programs' effectiveness and can make necessary adjustments to enhance their success and impact.

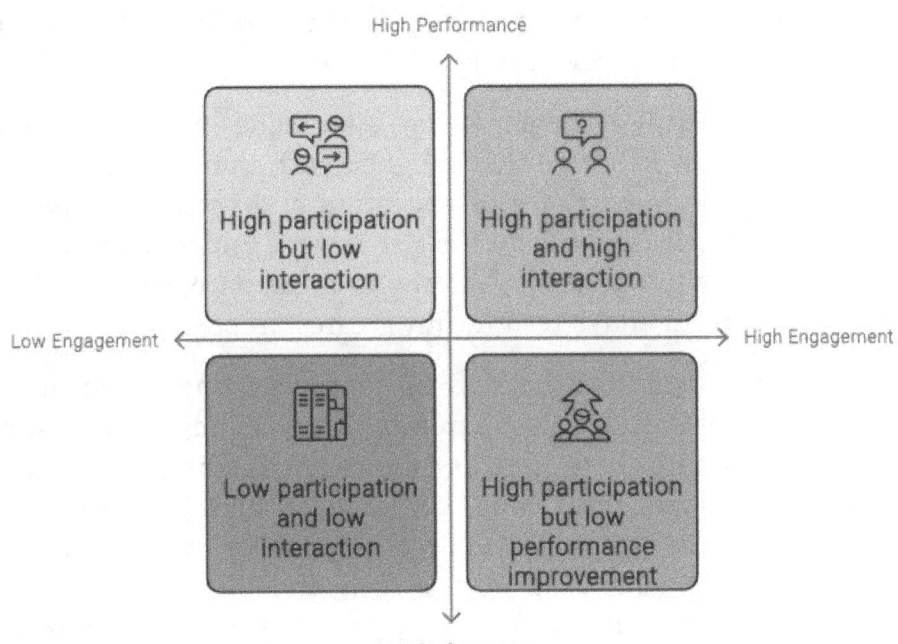

Enablement Program Effectiveness

CHAPTER 9

You & Enablement

"Enablement empowers individuals to reach their full potential, unlocking the value within themselves and driving success for the organization as a whole."

- **Passion**

My passion for empowering others developed through several steps:

First, I reflected on my own values and goals, and how helping others aligned with them. Recognizing the importance of education and personal growth, I felt compelled to assist others. Understanding my motivations allowed me to focus on what mattered most and determine my greatest impact.

I educated myself on various support theories and methods, exploring how individuals and groups can offer assistance. By reading books and papers, attending conferences and courses, and consulting with experts, I gained a comprehensive understanding of the field and identified specific approaches and techniques that suited my interests and objectives.

I actively sought opportunities to apply support in both my personal and professional life. Through these experiences, I honed my skills and discerned the positive impact of my efforts.

Continual reflection and learning from my experiences were essential. Regular self-assessments, soliciting feedback, and ongoing professional development activities enabled me to grow as an enabler and enhance the effectiveness and significance of my support initiatives.

Finding New Methods

Developing innovative teaching methods and maintaining learner engagement can propel careers in education or training. This passion involves exploring and experimenting with new instructional strategies that captivate, educate, and benefit learners.

To discover novel teaching methods and sustain engagement, staying informed on current research and trends in education and training is crucial. Engaging with academic literature, participating in conferences and workshops, and networking with fellow educators provide valuable insights. Keeping abreast of the latest developments in education allows for the application of cutting-edge techniques.

Openness to new ideas and perspectives is vital for uncovering fresh teaching approaches and ensuring learner engagement. This openness includes seeking feedback and suggestions from learners, colleagues, and experts while being willing to try previously unused methods. Embracing diverse viewpoints enhances the range and effectiveness of teaching strategies.

A genuine concern for student success drives the pursuit of innovative teaching methods. This dedication involves offering the necessary support, resources, and guidance for students to overcome challenges and achieve their goals. Those who prioritize student success create a conducive learning environment and assist learners in reaching their aspirations.

Listening

Listening to feedback is important for several reasons. Firstly, it reveals how others perceive us and our actions, highlighting areas for improvement.

Secondly, feedback provides insight into the impact of our actions on others, particularly when unintended consequences arise. By listening, we can learn from mistakes and make necessary adjustments.

Thirdly, considering feedback fosters strong relationships. Demonstrating openness to others' perspectives shows we value their input and are committed to collaboration and improvement.

Overall, listening to feedback enhances personal and professional relationships, driving greater effectiveness and success in achieving goals.

To understand employees' enablement needs, follow these steps:

Communicate your desire to understand staff requirements for better job performance. This can be done through emails, meetings, or visible notices, encouraging employees to share their thoughts and ideas.

Provide multiple channels for employees to communicate their enablement needs, such as dedicated email addresses, suggestion boxes, forums, or surveys and focus groups. Offering various options makes it easier for employees to provide feedback.

Actively listen to employees' concerns, asking questions for clarity and valuing their input. This openness demonstrates a commitment to addressing their needs.

Respond to employee feedback by providing updates and acting on their suggestions. Communicate progress and outcomes through regular updates, meetings, or digital platforms, showing your dedication to improving the organization based on their contributions.

Maintaining open dialogue about addressing employees' enablement needs underscores the company's commitment to their well-being and continuous improvement.

CHAPTER 10

Leading Enablement

Through my research and discussions with industry experts, it's become evident that enablement leaders need to possess robust leadership skills, including the ability to motivate and inspire others to achieve their objectives. These leaders must also excel in communication, articulating their team's goals and plans clearly. Effective enablement leaders should be adept listeners, considering diverse ideas and perspectives when making decisions. For a support team to function effectively, collaboration and active listening are essential.

These concepts underline the critical role of strong leadership in the sales training sector. By embodying the aforementioned skills and traits, enablement leaders can guide their teams towards success and drive positive changes within the company. Additionally, proficient leaders cultivate a positive and inclusive workplace environment. They act with fairness and consistency, fostering trust and teamwork among their team members.

Moreover, effective leaders manage their teams efficiently, ensuring alignment with shared goals. They delegate tasks and responsibilities appropriately, providing their teams with the necessary support and resources to succeed.

As a support leader, it is crucial to trust your team to act in the best interest of the organization. This involves granting them the autonomy and flexibility to develop and implement support programs and initiatives that align with the company's needs and objectives. By empowering enablement staff to make decisions and take action, you encourage innovation and enhance the success of the organization's enablement efforts.

Key Skills for Effective Enablement Leadership

There are a number of important reasons why enablement managers should trust their enablement staff to do what is best for the company.

- First, the people who work in enablement are usually experts in their fields. They have a lot of knowledge and experience in teaching and learning, as well as in the specific topics and areas that are important to the company. So, they are well-equipped to create and run effective enablement programs and projects that meet the goals and needs of the company.

- Second, enablement staff are frequently intimately aware of the requirements and concerns of the organization's workers, learners, and stakeholders. They talk to these groups often and know a lot about their goals, what drives them, and the problems they face. So, they are in a good position to make support programs and projects that fit the wants and desires of the organization's workers, learners, and stakeholders.

- Third, enablement workers are usually highly driven and committed to the organization's success. They are passionate about teaching and learning, and they want to help other people learn and grow. So, they are more likely to be involved and committed to their work and willing to put in the time and effort needed to create and implement effective enablement programs and projects.

CHAPTER 11

What if no enablement is done?

Case Study

A retail company had been open for more than 20 years and had earned a good name in its field. Even though the company was successful, confidence was low and there were a lot of people leaving.

The problem was that the company hadn't put any money into helping its salespeople do their jobs better. Sales reps didn't get enough training or help, so they often felt stressed and unprepared when they had to deal with customers. As a result, the sales reps found it hard to close deals and meet their sales goals, which made them angry and tired.

Even though the company's management team knew about the problems, they didn't think sales training was worth investing in. They thought that reps should be able to figure things out on their own and that training was a waste of time and money.

This choice had serious effects. Sales dropped by 25%, and the number of people leaving the company rose to more than 50%. The cost of constantly teaching and bringing on new sales reps was hurting the company's bottom line, which was a big worry.

When the management team at XYZ Inc. realized that not having sales support was hurting the business, they knew they had to do something. They started by looking closely at their sales process and figuring out where sales reps were having the most trouble.

- The company made a full sales training plan with several key parts based on this research: Training: The company spent money on a range of training programs for its sales reps, such as in-person classes, online courses, and one-on-one coaching. These schools put an emphasis on important skills like knowing about products, talking to customers, and dealing with objections.

- Tools and resources: The company also provided a variety of tools and resources to its reps to help them be more effective in their roles. Sales scripts, product guides, and customer relationship management software were all included.
- Support: So that reps could always get help and advice, the company set up a training program that put more experienced reps with less experienced reps. The mentors helped and gave tips on everything from how to make sales to how to handle your time.

The results of these attempts were very good. Within just a few months, sales started to go up and the number of people leaving the company went down by a lot. The company learned that investing in its employees was important for long-term success and that sales training was a key part of that equation..

Another study by LinkedIn found that sales reps stay with companies with good sales training programs 20% longer than those without good training programs.

Business Impact

It's hard to give specific examples of businesses that didn't empower employees because this is a subjective opinion that depends on the person and what they've been through. But there are some usual signs that a company isn't giving its staff what they need:

Lack of training and growth opportunities: A company that does not give employees the tools they need is not likely to give them chances to learn and grow. This could include failing to provide training programs, failing to provide access to educational tools, or failing to support workers who want to participate in professional development activities.

Few chances to move up: A company that doesn't give its workers the tools they need isn't likely to give them chances to grow or move up. This could mean not giving employees chances to take on new roles or tasks or not helping employees who want to change their careers.

Communication and feedback systems that don't work well: A company that doesn't give its employees a lot of freedom is unlikely to have good communication and feedback systems. This could mean not giving employees regular reviews of their work, not giving them helpful feedback, or not giving them the information and help they need to do their jobs well.

Lack of support and recognition: A company that does not enable its employees is unlikely to support and recognize its respective positions' efforts. This could mean not giving employees enough resources and support, not recognizing and rewarding them for their work, or not making the workplace a positive and encouraging place to be. If a company doesn't give its employees the tools they need to do their jobs, they are more inclined to practice undesirable behaviors that could impede their growth and development.

Customer Impact

When employees aren't given enough freedom, it can hurt the whole company. For example, if workers don't receive training effectively, they might make mistakes or take longer to finish tasks, which could lead to inefficiency and a loss of income. Also, if workers aren't engaged and driven, they may leave their jobs more often. This can cause the company to spend more money hiring and training new people. A lack of support can also lead to a bad work setting, which can hurt employee morale and make them less productive. In the long run, this can hurt the performance and effectiveness of the company as a whole.

CHAPTER 12

Selling Enablement Internally

Based on my reading and observations, it's evident that to sell enablement within a company, a transformation must take place. This builds internal support and buy-in for enablement projects, crucial for their success.

To establish strong backing, discuss the benefits of enablement with colleagues, highlighting improvements in sales team performance and overall company advantages.

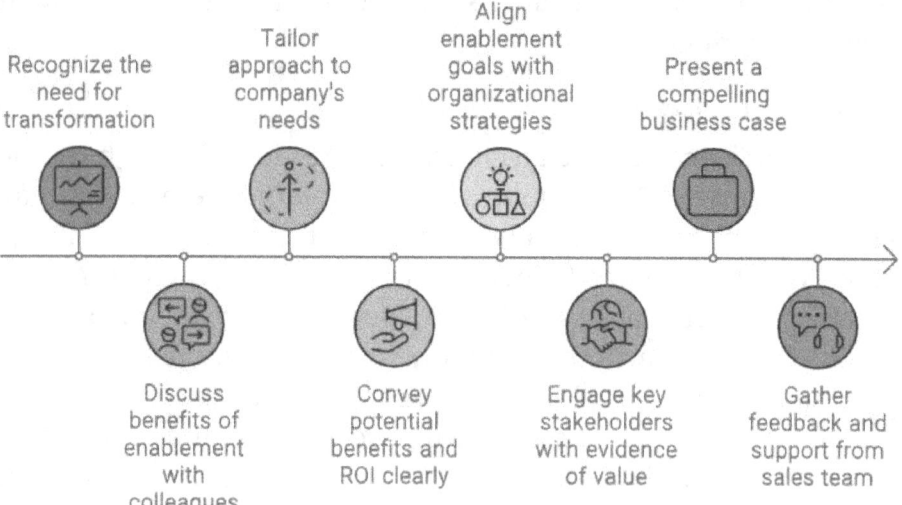

Secure Support and Funding for Sales Enablement

Recognize the need for transformation

Tailor approach to company's needs

Align enablement goals with organizational strategies

Present a compelling business case

Discuss benefits of enablement with colleagues

Convey potential benefits and ROI clearly

Engage key stakeholders with evidence of value

Gather feedback and support from sales team

Tactics for promoting enablement vary by organization. Understanding your company's needs and tailoring your approach is key. This garners support and accelerates enablement changes.

Conveying the potential benefits and ROI clearly can also secure essential tools and resources from key partners.

Align enablement goals with organizational strategies to ensure integration with core operations without seeming disconnected.

Ideas for increasing support and budget:

Engage key stakeholders with evidence of enablement's value through success stories and data on its impact.

Present a compelling business case detailing costs, benefits, and ROI, along with a thorough implementation plan.

Gather feedback and support from the sales team and staff via surveys or focus groups to understand their needs and suggestions.

Leverage external resources and experts, through consultations, workshops, or research, to strengthen your enablement proposition.

Be patient and persistent; gaining support and funding may take time and adjustment, but continuous advocacy and responsiveness are crucial.

With determination and flexibility, obtaining the necessary support for enablement is achievable.

CHAPTER 13

Reporting Structure

From the conversations I had, I discovered that the enablement organisational structure varies significantly depending on the company's size and requirements. Some interviewees noted that enablement functions as a separate entity reporting directly to the head of sales, while others stated it's integrated into a larger learning and development or training department.

One recurring theme was the critical importance of aligning enablement with the company's overall goals and objectives. Some respondents advocated for enablement to report to the Chief Revenue Officer or Chief Sales Officer to ensure proximity to the sales team. Others suggested that aligning under the Chief Marketing Officer or Chief Customer Officer could integrate sales support more closely with the organisation's broader marketing and customer experience initiatives.

Ultimately, the company's specific needs and objectives will dictate the optimal structure for enablement reporting. Collaborating and consulting with key stakeholders will be crucial in determining the best approach to support the company's success.

Whether or not to use a CLO

So that they can effectively handle and support the learning and growth of their workers. A chief learning officer (CLO) is a senior-level leader who is in charge of leading and managing the learning and development efforts of a company, as well as giving strategic direction and advice.

Large companies might need a CLO for a number of reasons, such as:

- To lead and guide learning and development efforts. A chief learning officer (CLO) can help create and implement a comprehensive and strategic approach to learning and development. They can also make sure that learning and development efforts are in line with the organization's overall business goals and objectives. This can help make sure that learning and development efforts are effective and efficient, and that they are focused on the organization's most important and urgent needs and goals.

- Coordinating and integrating learning and development efforts across the organization: A CLO can help coordinate and integrate learning and development efforts across different departments and functions. They can also make sure that all employees have access to the resources and support they need for learning and development. This can help break down silos within the organization and make it easier for people to work together and coordinate. It can also help make sure that the organization's learning and development efforts are uniform and well-coordinated.

- To help build a culture of learning: A chief learning officer (CLO) can help promote and advocate for learning and development within the company, as well as help build a culture of learning and development that never stops. This can mean getting involved with workers, letting them learn and grow in their jobs, and supporting the worth and benefits of learning and development. By creating a learning mindset, organizations can help their employees be more interested and committed to their jobs.

A CLO's specific responsibilities can vary depending on the

organization's size and needs, but some common duties and responsibilities may include:

- Creating and implementing the organization's learning and development strategy in accordance with the overall business goals and objectives.
- Collaborating with other leaders and stakeholders to identify and prioritize learning and development opportunities and needs.
- Creating and implementing learning and development programs and initiatives, such as workshops, seminars, e-learning courses, and other forms of learning.
- Evaluating the effectiveness of learning and development programs and making improvement recommendations
- Managing the learning and development budget and ensuring that learning and development efforts are delivered in a cost-effective and efficient manner.
- Actively promoting and advocating for learning and development within the organization, as well as fostering a culture of continuous learning and development.

In summary, the role of a chief learning officer (CLO) is to lead and guide the organization's learning and development efforts and make sure that employees have the skills, information, and assistance they need to do their jobs well.

CHAPTER 14

Points of Enablement Success

There are no silver bullets for success, but the ten suggestions below should get you launched.

1. Write down the exact goals and aims of your enablement program. This will help you make a program that fits the wants and goals of your company and is effective.

2. Make a central place for all material and tools related to sales. This makes it easy for sales teams to get to the information they need to do their jobs well.

3. Help sales teams get the information and skills they need to succeed by giving them training and help. This can include teaching and mentoring, as well as training on products, services, and sales processes.

4. Set up a way for employees to give comments and give you information. This can help you find places where your support program could be better and make the changes it needs.

5. Use statistics and analytics to track how well your program is working. This can help you figure out what is going well and what places might need more help.

6. Make sure you have a way to track and measure how well your sales training program is working. This can help you show how

valuable your program is and argue for more money to be put into it.

7. Work with other teams and departments, like marketing and product development, to make sure that your support program is in line with their efforts and goals.

8. Give your sales teams regular information and contact to keep them up-to-date on your program and interested in it. Provide ongoing support and resources to assist sales teams in developing and improving over time.

9. Evaluate and change your support program on a regular basis to make sure it stays effective and meets the changing needs of your business and sales teams.

CHAPTER 15

The Future of Enablement

As I sat in my office, I couldn't help but contemplate what the future of enablement might look like. Changes in technology, changes in the business world, and changes in how learning and development methods are used would all have an effect.

But as I thought about it, I began to recognize a few trends and changes that stood out as especially important. One trend that seemed likely to keep going was the growing use of technology and digital media in enabling. With how quickly technology is changing, people who work in enablement would have access to a growing number of tools and networks they could use to make learning experiences that are interesting and effective. Artificial intelligence (AI) and natural language processing (NLP) systems that are more advanced and virtual reality (VR) and augmented reality (AR) technologies could all be added to the mix.

Another trend that seemed likely to shape the future of support was a greater focus on personalized and individualized learning experiences. As the workforce became more diverse and workers' learning styles and tastes changed, enablement practitioners had to offer learning experiences that were tailored to each person's needs. This could be done by using data and analytics to figure out each employee's skills and flaws and then giving them learning opportunities that are tailored to their needs.

Lastly, the continuing trend toward online work and flexible work plans was also expected to have an effect on the future of support. As more and more people worked from home or other faraway places, enablement professionals had to find ways to make learning easy and useful in a wide range of scenarios. This could mean using digital platforms and technologies to set up virtual learning settings and coming up with ways to help remote workers and make sure they have the information and skills they need to do their jobs well.

At the end I was sure that the future of enablement would be shaped by changes in technology, personalized and individualized learning experiences, and the growing trend toward working remotely. And, as an enablement practitioner, I was thrilled to be a part of it all and to see where the adventure would lead us next.

CHAPTER 16

Final thoughts

When I sat down to write this book, I had a clear idea of what I wanted to do. I wanted to learn more about enablement and how it can help businesses succeed in today's competitive market.

But as I dug deeper into my research and started writing, I quickly learned that I had a lot to learn. I tried to learn as much as I could by reading a lot of books, talks, and case studies.

When I started talking to people who knew a lot about the subject, I really started to learn. These people were able to give useful insights and examples of how business support had helped their organizations.

Through these talks, I learned how important it is to give workers a lot of freedom, encourage teamwork, and push for new ideas. I learned that successful business support requires a diverse approach that includes technology, training, culture, and communication, among other things.

As I wrote, I found myself using what I had learned about company support in my own work. I saw how giving my team more responsibility and using new tools could make us more efficient and productive. Writing this book also made me understand how important it is for my company to be innovative. I started to think of new ways to solve problems and improve processes, and I told my team to do the same. This change in our way of thinking helped our work, and we were able to come up with new and creative ideas that set us apart in our field.

Overall, writing this book was a life-changing experience that not only let me share my study and thoughts with others but also helped me grow and develop as a professional. I'm glad that writing this book gave me the chance to learn so much, and I can't wait to use what I've learned in my work life.

As a worker in the field of enablement, I have had the chance to see how fulfilling this job can be. I've had the chance to help other people learn and grow, as well as give them the support and tools they need to be successful.

One of the best parts of my job has been getting to work with people from different backgrounds. I have worked with employees from different areas and levels of the company as well as learners from a wide range of backgrounds and experiences. This has helped me understand different points of view and ways of doing things and learn from the experiences of others.

I have also had the chance to be artistic and try new things with how I teach and how I learn. I've used many different tools, methods, and techniques to get students interested and help them learn in new and interesting ways. This has kept students interested and driven, which has made learning more effective and fun.

At the end of the day, empowerment is a job that involves working with people and can have a long-term effect on their lives and jobs. As an enablement professional, it is satisfying to be able to add to the organization's general success and well-being. "Leadership is about making it possible for others to act," says the quote, and I'm glad that my job gives me the chance to do that.

www.ingramcontent.com/pod-product-compliance
Lightning Source LLC
Chambersburg PA
CBHW070606220526
45467CB00003B/1318